BUYER AGENT BE AWARE
by Allan Dalton

with contributions by

Cristal Clarke, Emmett Laffey, Kathleen Rebhan,

Teresa Palacios Smith, Maxwell Stevens, Julie Vanderblue,

and Andrew Undem

For all inquiries, bulk discounts, and more contact — thomasryanward@gmail.com

Covers, Graphic Design and Layout by Thomas Ryan Ward

All images provided by Canva.com and its contributors.

ISBN 9798324456023

Printed in the United States of America.

DEDICATION

Although I would like to be original and dedicate a book to someone who has never had a book dedicated to them before, that would deprive me of dedicating **BUYER AGENT BE AWARE** to the real estate industry's uncontested G.O.A.T. (Greatest Of All Time).

Gino Blefari was recently ranked by Swanepoel Power 200 as the Real Estate Industry's #1 Leader. Ostensively, because of his most notable achievements across a wide range of real estate positions.

Gino was the number one producing real estate agent in ultra-competitive Santa Clara County (with approximately 2M residents). He went on to become the president of the number one Century 21 brokerage in the world (where 7 of the 11 top global network offices were his). He then founded Intero Real Estate Services (one of the most successful brokerages in the world). From there, Gino became CEO (and later Chairman) of Berkshire Hathaway HomeServices and is presently CEO of HomeServices of America.

Gino, widely respected for this commitment to the community and charities, was honored and feted as the Italian American Businessperson of the Year and was also instrumental in founding and sustaining The Intero Foundation – one of metropolitan San Jose's leading charities.

Gino, a devoted husband, proud father of two accomplished daughters, and beloved pet owner of 'June', is noted for his ability to help individuals and groups to maximize their professional and personal potential... and does so in a highly respectful, humane, caring, and collaborative matter.

There is no one in the real estate industry that I have ever admired as much.

BUYER AGENT BE AWARE was earnestly and passionately conceived, written, and produced to guide and aid Buyer Agents and brokerages as they assume the full responsibility of better determining, defining, and presenting their individually negotiated Buyer-side fees and relevant value... to increasingly informed, value-seeking and cost-conscious Buyers.

———·✧·———

DISCLAIMER

BUYER AGENT BE AWARE is not associated with any Brand, Brokerage, or real estate association. The book intends to make available innovative yet practical 'How-to' Buyer Agent-related messaging, suggestions, systems and services greatly needed in a post-real estate disrupted environment, and should not be viewed in any way as 'official policy' or one-size-fits-all dogma.

Rather, the curriculum and content provided by the author and the highly accomplished real estate buyer agent contributors and industry leaders are designed to stimulate individual and group reflection. Self-reflection and group discussion are necessary for individuals to determine how they intend to best serve the Buyer Clients they represent.

The publisher and the author are providing this book and its contents on an 'as is' basis and make no representations or warranties of any kind in respect to this book and its contents. The publisher and the author do not make any guarantee or promise as to any results obtained from using the content of this book... and assume no responsibilities for any inaccuracies, errors, or omissions.

BUYER AGENT BE AWARE
'Circle of Content'

Elevating **Buyer Agent Value** Through ***BUYER AGENT BE AWARE***

THE WHY · 7 A's Buyer Agent Presentation · Open House Buyers · CRM · A.I. · New Construction Buyers · Co-Brokerage · Renter to Buyer System · RELO & Out-of-Area Buyers · Resort & 2nd Home Buyers · Luxury Buyers · 1st Time Buyers · Home Buying System · Community Videos · Buyer Divisions · Social Media · Content · Broker Perspective · Fair Housing Buyers · Much More

TABLE OF CONTENTS

A Pre-Introductory Bonus

Throughout this book/resource, there are innumerable examples of where conventional real estate practices and calcified cliches are challenged, corrected, or converted to more contemporaneously relevant and client-centric levels of communication. As a precursor to what the reader can expect throughout this Socratic method of learning, **BUYER AGENT BE AWARE** begins with some of the author's most notable examples (Dalton's Don'ts and Do's) of how many of the industry's most commoditized methods of communication can be significantly improved.

DON'T	DO
Say listing presentation	Say marketing proposal
Say, "Homes don't sell because of price!"	Say, "Homes don't sell because of ineffective marketing... because price is part of marketing."
Say, my Past Clients	Say, my Clients for Life
Treat your business like a business	Treat your business like a professional practice because businesses have customers and practices have Clients
Just talk about data bases	Think client bases
Refer to "listing agents"	Refer to "seller agents"
Think recruiting	Think selection
Think retention	Think development

DON'T	DO
Call where you work "an office"	Call where you work "a regional sales and marketing center"
Just serve your community	Represent your community as its town storyteller
Just use ChatGPT to praise the home for your seller	Also use A.I. to critique homes and towns when negotiating for your Buyer
Ever ask a homeseller, "When would you like to get started?"	Ask the homeseller, "How soon would you like your magnificent home sold to the 'right buyer'?"
Tell a For Sale By Owner they cannot sell their home	Tell them you can market and network their home
Recommend a price to a homeseller	Discuss different pricing strategies
Say when asked, "How is the market?" ..."That depends on if you are a buyer, seller, or investor."	"Thanks for asking. We're in an opportunistic market." Then review the opportunities for each sector and answer the question, rather than throwing the question back at them. No one likes when a question isn't honored and they are subjected to blatant evasiveness. Like when people ask, "Does the home have four bedrooms," and the response is, "Do you want four bedrooms?" because this trite response was featured in their training program.

DON'T	DO
Ever justify your value because of your service	Validate your value because of your service, service(s), skills and results
Ever state on the back of your business card, "The sincerest compliment someone can pay me is to send me referrals from their friends and family."	Announce, "My greatest professional privilege is to serve the real estate needs of one's friends and families."
Ever advertise: When you are ready to buy or sell, give me a call.	Advertise: When you are "considering" buying, selling, or home improvement, give me a call.
Ever brag and say, "I am number one," and leave it at that.	Say, "I was number one this year, but I know that means nothing to you unless I get you the best results. So, let me share how I plan to do that."
Ever put down a competitor	Say, "They are a great company and are an important part of my marketing system."
Ever promote that you attend conventions	Announce that you represented your area at a convention
Ever just announce awards and accomplishments	Add to the end, this ... "because my clients deserve the very best."
Ask visitors to open houses to sign in	Learn how to have them sign out

DON'T	DO
Ever say your company opened up a new office in town	Say, "When people think of (name of town), they think of (your company)." Do this from day one.
Waste a billboard or social media platform by promoting yourself	Combine messages, "Allan Dalton sells America's #1 lifestyle… Fairfield County!" All homeowners will thank you.
Just ask consumers whom you engage, "Thinking of buying or selling?"	Say, "I would love for you to become one of my clients (even if you have never met them before)."
Ever say, "My clients are getting divorced".	Unless you can accurately add, "…and they have authorized me to say this."
Just ask a home seller what they love about the home	Say, "Now that we have reviewed all the reasons why buyers would love this home, is there anything that you think a buyer or buyer agent might criticize that we should discuss tonight?" (These last two gems are courtesy of Julie Vanderblue).
Do real estate seminars	Real estate town meetings (included in this book)

DON'T

Ask people for their loyalty

Talk about qualifying the buyer

Ever say to your home sellers, "The buyers want a home with more privacy (etc.)."

Call homes: beautiful, charming, gracious, spacious, or elegant, or has magnificent views (or the same things a pizza delivery person might say about the home when delivering, "beautiful home," to get a bigger tip).

Say you sell more homes

Say you do a buyer's CMA

DO

Thank them for their loyalty

Say, "Let's establish your purchasing power!"

Say (if true), "I have received a lot of wonderful compliments, but unfortunately, buyers do not want to go over 800K, even for homes that are as highly appealing as yours."

(my favorite): "Your amazing home enjoys views and vistas that even Ernest Hemingway could not adequately describe."

Say your mission, when representing home sellers, is to sell homes for more

Say, "Most agents merely do a CMA which just provides an estimate of market value. Instead, you do an MMA (merchandising market analysis) which also shows what they can do to add value to the home, and how you can advise and arrange for this.

DON'T	DO
When homeowners proudly point out improvements, don't just say how impressive the improvements are.	Say, "What you did is really going to provide us with a marketing advantage, and whose idea was it to make these improvements?"
Just praise an estate	Say, "Folks, I am very comfortable in a home of this aesthetic grandeur, because I grew up in a similar size home. Although I must say, there were six other families living with us."
Say how you are different	Say, "Rather than focusing on how I am different, I always focus on what makes your home and lifestyle different. You see, I don't compete against other agents as much as I cooperate to get homes sold. But your home will compete against other homes in the market, so my focus is on your home's competitive advantage and not mine. But when pressed, I acknowledge that I am in the top one to five percent of producing agents in the industry, although I know that means nothing to you unless we get you the best results."

DON'T	DO
Say, "Let's look at similar homes."	Say, "Let's take a look at properties that buyers will be evaluating at the same time they are evaluating your home."
Say, "How are you going to select an agent?"	Say, "What would you expect from me as your agent?"
Say, "You should not be at home during showings."	Say, "Don't be at home during showings unless I think there would be a natural connection between you and the buyers."
Just praise home features	Say, "Don't be at home during showings unless I think there would be a natural connection between you and the buyers."
Just praise home features	Praise the home seller for also selecting the features
Tell a home seller that you will, "Give that price a try."	Say, "I will aggressively fight for that price, but if the response is unfavorable, we will have to make an immediate price adjustment."

DON'T	DO
Say, "Either the market or the buyer determines the price." Then why do they need you?	Say, "The market only influences the price. What determines the price is the buyer, the buyer agent, the seller, the seller agent, the lender, the appraiser, and the appeal of the home."
Place buyers and sellers in personality or behavioral boxes without their taking a personality test.	Look at people as individuals and not as categories, and ask the appropriate questions in order to identify idiosyncrasies.
Use the word 'Commission' as it refers only to a sale.	Say 'Fee' as in 'attorney fees' expresses a level of value that goes beyond the transaction and includes professional advice.

That is enough for now.

Let me know if you like any of my suggestions:
AllanDaltonConsulting@gmail.com

PROLOGUE

(for the more strategic readers only)
These opening thoughts do not provide any immediate answers to post-real estate disruption, as do the following segments of How-To's that follow, but for those who also focus and speculate as to the long-term future of Buyer Agent value, this prologue is intended for you.

BUYER AGENT VALUE MUST PUT AN END TO 'PAST CLIENTS'

Years ago, while CEO of Realtor.com, when speaking to real estate groups, I would often introduce two interrelated concepts, which, if employed today, could significantly empower Buyer Agents to elevate their value with Buyer Clients.

I did so by merging the real estate industry's need to purge the value-destroying expression 'my Past Clients' while providing real estate professionals the opportunity to encourage and guide real estate consumers to thoughtfully develop their own real estate and financially related goals. My **Real Estate Financial Planning System**, which I developed during my earlier days as a co-owner of a major regional brokerage (and a program no longer available but referenced here for illustrative purposes) introduced a new real estate concept. The proposed paradigm shift, at that time, was intended to help our fifty-plus real estate offices and approximately two thousand associates to communicate and provide greater value to consumers and Clients.

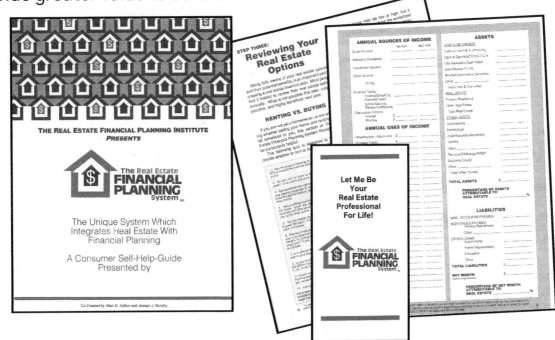

Another of my intentions was to address, with irrefutable logic, that if my associates considered former Clients as 'Past Clients', then their 'Past Clients' must be considering them as 'Past Agents'.

Should real estate brokerages, teams, and individual Buyer Agents decide to develop their updated and digital version of this real estate and finance-related concept, it might also stimulate additional methods of how real estate value is being communicated. Perhaps CRMs would not only represent **Contact Management Systems** but also **Client Management Systems**. That Buyer Agents would not only talk in terms of **databases** but also **Client Bases**. By doing so, real estate professionals would be encouraged to not only treat their **business like a business** but also as a **professional practice**... since **businesses have customers** and **practices have Clients**. That real estate professionals would not just think of SOI as sphere of influence' but also how to better influence their sphere. Converting real estate customers to Buyer Clients and sustaining them as Clients for life is precisely what other professional practices do!

I named my program **The Real Estate Financial Planning System** in recognition that every real estate transaction also possesses a financial component. Additionally, after considering how thirty real estate agents were in a hotel break-out room learning how to best make a listing presentation, several hundred consumers simultaneously were in the hotel's ballroom learning how to best invest in real estate. The beauty of my system was that **it was a self-help guide**, one that did not require any additional certification on behalf of the real estate agent providing the information. Moreover, and by design, within The Real Estate Financial Planning System guide, to avoid any potential liability for our associates or our company, the only advice is that consumers should develop their own plan. This decades ahead-of-its-time program elevated conventional 'farming' methods within our company and re-defined the professional intentions and essence of our associates.

I am re-visiting this concept in 2024 in the belief that unless Buyer Agents convey to prospective Buyer Clients that they hope to provide real estate trusted advice that includes financial strategies and preparation to both acquire real estate and increase property value after acquisition, then, Buyer Agent value becomes limited to the transaction.

The real estate industry is not alone in how it must adjust its business model, after being partially disrupted. The best explanation of disruption that I have heard, is "Disruption takes place when something no longer makes sense." Years ago, someone outside of the life insurance industry, Ralph Nader, attacked that industry's conventional approach of disproportionately promoting **cash-value life insurance**. The selling of cash-value life insurance enabled life insurance agents to earn higher commissions. This disruption not only led to the greater emergence of **term insurance** but also was the catalyst that witnessed life insurance Agents evolving into **financial planners**.

Real estate agents and companies, however, will never need to change their professional name because the product they sell and market will remain the same. What will change, in my opinion, is the prosperity achieved in the coming years for top-producing agents and brokerages... provided there are proper adjustments. Top Agents and brokerages will continue to flourish, deservedly so. Not just because large numbers of real estate agents, who are unable to convince consumers of their indispensable value, will leave the industry.

The more accomplished real estate professionals (just like the elite contributors featured on the back of this book) will also now enjoy a more expanded opportunity to present their negotiated fee value. This will occur as Buyer Clients become compelled to select their Buyer Agent more judiciously.

"What's in a name?"

Value-rich Buyer Agent Proposals, where Buyer Agents explain their 'before, during, and after the transaction importance', including the possibility of introducing the offer of lifetime trusted advice, will result in the following positive consequences:

1) When a **Client-for-Life Proposal** is established, either during or after the Buyer Agent presentation (yet before an agreed contract is signed, or at the very least when this subject is broached) it can lead to enviable consequences. This **offer of value** after and well beyond the transaction provides a Buyer with a choice. A choice to either acknowledge that they approve of receiving lifetime value and, if not, to at least agree to sign up to have their immediate needs served. By explaining to the prospective Buyer Client, during this consultative process and presentation, that you want to do such a great job for them that they will want you to serve them for years to come (although this might be getting ahead of itself) also conveys that you have more than this one transaction at stake. Thus, you hope to have them as a Client-for-Life.

2) Another benefit of your revealing, during a consultation, that your spirit of intent is to provide **after the sale value** demonstrates why you have Lifetime Clients and the respect you enjoy in the community... and that you have developed mutual respect amongst the all-important home service tradespeople and providers.

3) That Buyers will understand that their Buyer Agent will also be involved in their ongoing need for home maintenance referrals, home improvement consultations and referrals, market updates, and the possibility of real estate investment strategies.

Another important shift in Buyer Agent-related Value is when exponentially greater Buying-side Value is more greatly emphasized and attributed to exceptional skills, deep market knowledge, and employment of systems, services, and solutions that are so valuable that they transcend the importance of personal service (as necessary and appreciated as that may be).

Regarding the relative value of skills, market knowledge, and trusted advice when compared to great personal service, please consider something I once came across. It was an immigration form that asked prospective citizens to America to check off their occupation on one of two lists. One list was titled 'Skilled Professionals' and the other 'Service Workers'. Listed in the 'Skills Section' were the following examples among dozens of others:

Skill Sector occupations and professions:
Attorneys, Financial Advisors, Doctors, Engineers, Plumbers, Electricians, Management Personnel, Pilots, Psychologists, Counsellors, Teachers, etc.

Service Sector jobs:
Waiters (today would be Servers), Housecleaners, Hotel Workers, Retail Salespeople, Real Estate Salespeople, Insurance Salespeople (and dozens of others).

What I inferred, after studying this list and noting that my career came from both sectors (and we cannot thank enough the service providers who keep the country operating effectively and vitally), were these conclusions:

Skilled occupations represented individuals who had to 'create work' of their own. Work that required greater critical thinking, organization, a much higher degree of training and education, more advisory, more complex, and less replaceable. Society could not function without full representation from each sector. Yet I can think of no other profession that better reflects the characteristics associated with the Skills Sector than a real estate professional. One who must manage immense complexity, possess multi-dimensional skills, knowledge of technology, marketing, networking, negotiation, market data, artificial intelligence, social media marketing, and social skills. Add to that, conflict resolution, amazing energy, collaboration, and all while working on a contingency fee with no guarantee of compensation.

Real estate professionals do more and receive less credit than any other skill sector worker when comprehensively compared.

Have you ever wondered why respect for real estate professionals does not equate to true value? One of many simple explanations is by pointing to how some agents, when challenged on their value, will spontaneously respond by saying, "But I give better service." That well-intentioned and seemingly defensive response does not begin to capture the immense value and professional preparation required of a professional real estate agent. Not only does the proclamation that one 'gives better service' not provide a clue as to what that means, but it ignores the importance of much higher related areas of value as seen in my real estate value pyramid.

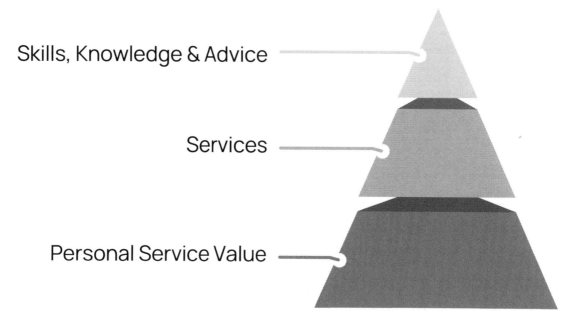

Skills, Knowledge & Advice

Services

Personal Service Value

At the bottom of the pyramid is Personal Service value, taken directly from the service sector. In the middle is "Services" and not service, as professional services represent the value bridge between the service sector and skills sector. At the peak of the pyramid is where skill, knowledge, and advice take overwhelming precedence. The reason the knowledge and skill level transcends both personal service and even professional service(s) is that, post **real estate disruption**, continuing to expect consumers to pay Buyer Agents 'surgeon skill-level fees' in the name of 'great service' will be futile.

In the following segment, you will learn of **The 7 A's of Buyer Agent Value Presentation**. You will be asked to insert, at various levels within this format, your most important home-related services, your transaction management systems, your commitment to personal service, and how you employ your market knowledge, experience, and especially your communication skills, in connection with how you describe each of **The 7 A's of Buyer Agent Value**.

Specifically, how you explain:

1) Agency

2) How you skillfully provide Access

3) How you skillfully Arrange on-and-off-market Access to properties

4) How you Apprise Buyers of existing home values as well as how to increase the value of a home they may buy and how you effectively negotiate for them

5) How you Answer all questions based on your knowledge and the trusted informational resources you can access

6) How you will professionally 'Administer' the transaction, including all of the necessary mortgage, title, insurance, inspections, and documents which you will tell me whether you want to receive either digitally or physically

7) How the 'After the Sale Value' you provide will be enormously beneficial... and possibly even explain how you would like to provide free, ongoing consulting and help them develop and execute their future real estate plans.

To that end, I respectfully invite you (after reviewing and possibly re-reading this book, one intended as an ongoing resource for Buyer Agents) to please consider encouraging your friends and colleagues (even if only those out of your market) to acquire this book.

The more that Buyer Agents are exposed to new ideas (or the resurgence of older but more timely than ever ideas) and exposed to the Buyer Agent Methods of the real estate legends featured in this book, the more that the industry as a whole (and especially the Clients that Buyer Agents "skillfully" advise and serve) will significantly benefit.

Thank you for your kind attention,

Allan Dalton
allandaltonconsulting@gmail.com

SEGMENT 1

DEFINING YOUR BUYER AGENT VALUE

DEVELOPING YOUR BUYER AGENT PRESENTATIONAL VALUE

DISTRIBUTING YOUR BUYER AGENT VALUE

There is a world of difference between presenting a Buyer Agreement **where the Buyer pays a negotiated fee** <u>versus</u> when **Buyers are not asked to pay a fee.**

95% of Marketing Presentations are about **the Value the Agent brings** with 5% being about the fee.

95% of the Buyer Agreement Presentation should be about **value to the Buyer...** and only 5% discussing the negotiated fee.

Buyer Value must first be identified before negotiated fees can be discussed.

The greater your Buyer Value Presentation is the easier it will be to have your negotiated fee accepted ... otherwise, you are left with trying to justify mathematically the itemized and individual Value of everything you do ... **which is very difficult if not impossible.**

The following content comprehensively reviews how to establish and communicate what you believe is your true and "individual" Value to Buyers and to execute compensated Buyer Agreements.

Determining Buyer Agent Value

With very little warning or preparation in 2024 / 2025, much of the real estate industry finds itself challenged in a way that it has never been before. Specifically, the predicament is to persuade real estate Buyers that they must now directly pay a transactional fee. This transformation requires the serious and strategic attention of brokerages and agents in order to resolve the following three issues:

1. What do you need to do to validate the negotiated fees you hope to charge?

2. How do you best communicate Buyer-side Value?

3. To what degree, if any, do you market or publicize:
    A . Your Buyer-side Value (beyond our inventory of homes)
    B . Your companies individually selected fees

Exercises / Discussions

Although each of the following activities is most relevant, and in some cases indispensable in order to help Buyer Agents consummate a transaction, it is important to contextualize each deliverable.

Please Customize the Pie Chart to Determine the Following:

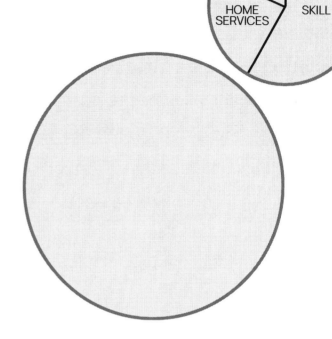

Example

SERVICE

HOME SERVICES

SKILL

1) Decide which % of your value to home sellers is due to **professional skills**.

2) Decide which % is due to your **personal services**.

3) What % is due to the **services you arrange or facilitate**.

While your percentages are surely estimates, this exercise will cause you to focus on the importance of each and how it is difficult to achieve full value without delivering value to Clients within each of these three all-important real estate realms.

Now please customize this next pie chart to reflect your "estimated" **value to Buyers?**

The reason this exercise is so important and relevant is that the word "service" for many real estate professionals applies only to the notion of **providing personal service** rather than representing **home services**.

Again real estate professionals universally when stating "they give great service" is akin to how everyone in prison claims "they are innocent!" It is completely and **universally expected and repeated**.

Is it really possible to provide "great service" without including a number of home services? Services that are **not personally delivered** but arranged by you as part of one's personal and professional **real estate ecosystem**.

Let's further examine the three dimensions of value highlighted in a value pyramid: skills, service, and services.

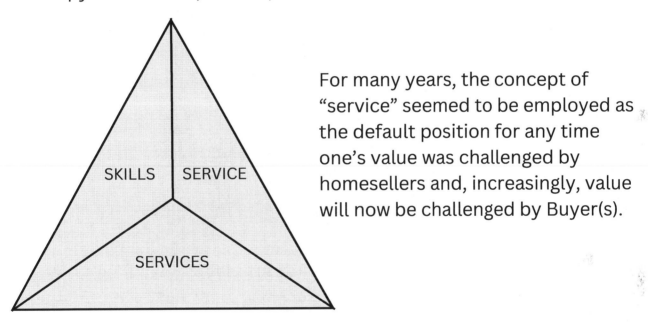

For many years, the concept of "service" seemed to be employed as the default position for any time one's value was challenged by homesellers and, increasingly, value will now be challenged by Buyer(s).

Seller: Why should we select you over _____?

Agent: Because I will give you the best service!

Seller: The other agent will charge us less.

Agent: But I give better service!

Service

"We make a living by what we get, we make a life by what we give."

Winston Churchill

<u>Less relied upon was:</u>

Agent: Because I have greater skills regarding negotiating, staging, marketing, and networking!

Seller: I have a million-dollar home. What is your fee?

[Agent introduces that fees are negotiable and suggests a fee]

Seller: My son has a $100K home. What will you charge him?

Agent: The same fee.

Seller: Will you also give him excellent service?

Agent: Yes!

Seller: Why do I pay ten times as much for the same "great service"?

Validating Value Based Upon Skills

Agent: Because my skills are <u>ten times more valuable</u> on a million-dollar home. My **negotiating skills**, I believe, are worth at least one point and they are worth ten times as much.

<u>Moreover even less said was:</u>

Agent: The reason, I believe, I am worth more is that **my staging skills** and **value** are worth at least another point on a million-dollar home which is worth ten times more to you... than on a hundred-thousand-dollar home.

This example illustrates that, at times, many Agents rely on attempting to "justify their value" based upon vague references to "superior service" because they could not guarantee results and were not able to communicate the value of their skills in a cogent manner.

Even less focus, for many, was the introduction of their ongoing value associated with being a "home services provider" or conduit.

Agent: The home services value I can provide through my company's real estate network of vendors will be indispensable and invaluable to you both now **and for years to come!**

Now that homeowners remain in their homes for up to 13 years (versus 7 or 8 in the past) means that real estate, lifestyle planning, and home services represent unprecedented value. **They are vital in three ways:**

1) Closing the loyalty gap (thank you, Chris Stuart)

2) Converting past Clients into Clients-for-Life

3) Merging skills, personal service, and home services

List all of the real estate-related services you provide homesellers:

1 _____ 6 _____

2 _____ 7 _____

3 _____ 8 _____

4 _____ 9 _____

5 _____ 10 _____

Now please list every home related service you provide or suggest to Buyers during a transaction:

1 _____ 6 _____

2 _____ 7 _____

3 _____ 8 _____

4 _____ 9 _____

5 _____ 10 _____

Which programs would add value to...

Homesellers:

1 _____   6 _____

2 _____   7 _____

3 _____   8 _____

4 _____   9 _____

5 _____   10 _____

Homeowners:

1 _____   6 _____

2 _____   7 _____

3 _____   8 _____

4 _____   9 _____

5 _____   10 _____

Buyers:

1 _____   6 _____

2 _____   7 _____

3 _____   8 _____

4 _____   9 _____

5 _____   10 _____

Questions to Consider or Discuss

1) What do you think is more important to Buyers, your...

Skills ☐

Personal Service ☐

Providing Home-related Services ☐

2) What do you think your most valuable skill is?

_____

3) What service are you providing that you did not provide on the past?

_____

4) Do you provide mortgage referrals to your Buyers?   YES NO

5) How do you communicate this to Buyers?

_____

6) Do you recommend insurance providers?   YES NO

7) How many business building partners are you now using?

1 _____   6 _____

2 _____   7 _____

3 _____   8 _____

4 _____   9 _____

5 _____   10 _____

8) Describe the relationship between providing home services and being a trusted real estate advisor:

_____

_____

_____

1. Locate properties for sale online.

       1   2   3   4   5

Can Buyers perform this task on their own?   YES   NO

2. Possess deep market and property knowledge.

       1   2   3   4   5

Do most Buyers possess this knowledge?   YES   NO

3. Arrange showings.

       1   2   3   4   5

Will most Buyers be able or willing to do this?   YES   NO

4. Knock on doors or call homeowners whose homes are not on the market.

       1   2   3   4   5

Will most Buyers conduct this assertive activity?   YES   NO

5. Know of properties that were taken off the market and why.

   1   2   3   4   5

Do most Buyers possess this knowledge?   Y E S   N O

6 . Your knowledge of construction and home improvement.

   1   2   3   4   5

Do most Buyers possess this knowledge including   Y E S   N O
resale implications of home improvement?

7. Knowledge of neighborhoods, schools, services, safety, transportation, etc.

   1   2   3   4   5

Do most Buyers have this knowledge?   Y E S   N O

8. The ability to negotiate for a better price and terms.

   1   2   3   4   5

Do most Buyers have this ability especially considering
every time they offer or counter their position weakens?   Y E S   N O

9. Your knowledge and connections with mortgage, insurance, title, and
appraisers.

   1   2   3   4   5

Do most Buyers have this knowledge and contacts?   Y E S   N O

10. Your ability to administrate the transactional process from writing the offer to closing.

        1   2   3   4   5

Do most Buyers possess this ability?   Y E S   N O

11. To resolve maintenance negotiations effectively.

        1   2   3   4   5

Do most Buyers possess this skill or are they able
to even do this comfortably?   Y E S   N O

12. Ability to navigate and negotiate through complex multi-offer scenarios.

        1   2   3   4   5

Do most Buyers possess the desire or skill in this
highly sophisticated task?   Y E S   N O

Others: Please add other important skills or services that you provide that most Buyers either do not want to do or cannot.

13. _____

      1   2   3   4   5

14. _____

      1   2   3   4   5

15. _____

      1   2   3   4   5

16. _____

      1   2   3   4   5

17. _____

      1   2   3   4   5

18. _____

      1   2   3   4   5

19. _____

      1   2   3   4   5

20. _____

      1   2   3   4   5

DEVELOPING YOUR BUYER AGENT PRESENTATION

Now that you have concluded which services and skills you score the highest, along with the ones where the Buyers do not, and where they are least proficient or prepared, you are now ready to prepare to build your buying side presentation.

Cautionary note: Although the real estate industry is renowned for its obsession with scripts dictated by others, the best presentations are ones where you manifest observable comfort and authenticity. Therefore, I will now present a series of concepts and thoughts that might assist you as you construct the individualized way in which you communicate Buying-side Value. This process should lead to a Buyer Agency contract being signed.

Again, it is not my role and not permissible for me to attempt to influence the type of Buyer-side contracts you construct or how your contracts deal with length of agreement, geography, fee, or any other factors or conditions contained within a Buyer Agreement Contract. The design and description of contracts are obviously, clearly, and "exclusively" your domain. What is incontrovertibly permissible as a consultant, is to share some general advice in the areas of gaining trust, and the keys to making compelling, persuasive, and interactive Buyer-side Presentations.

For those of you familiar with my work, you will not be surprised that for the sake of presentational memorization, I like to employ alliteration.
Some initial thoughts regarding presenting value to Buyers.

Some initial thoughts regarding presenting Value to Buyers

Please remember that the more information in the form of text and video that a Buyer receives from you (before you speak or meet) the higher the level of credibility and trust will be established before you begin your value presentation and Buyer agreement process.

I want to offer an important premise for my proposed presentation showcased below. It is designed to show your value, cause a Buyer to accept a negotiated fee, and sign a contract. This recommended approach deliberately does not comprehensively cover all of the fact-finding Buyer needs or their objectives. This is because I am assuming that this interpersonal process has already been performed innumerable times by most real estate agents when working with Buyers, and consequently this process requires very little of my perspective or new recommendations.

Instead, my focus will primarily and parenthetically be devoted to recommending approaches regarding achieving signed Buyer Agreements, where Buyer Agents are compensated directly by the Buyer. Please note that this following presentation draws upon the value checklist I outlined earlier.

Dalton's 7-A's Buyer Presentation

(For those Agents who want to demonstrate twice as much value as AAA Service!)

"Folks, I have found it helpful for my Buyer Clients to follow what I do for them, by breaking down my representational value into steps. Each step in my representational process begins with the letter A."

7 A's disk design of my concept was created by Brian Bilek
and provided to **BUYER AGENT BE AWARE** courtesy of Emmet Laffey

Agency

"Years ago, folks, Buyer Agents had no representation as the agent they were working with in most cases was a sub-agent to the home seller. Today I am happy to say that many Buyers have full agency representation. Now, just as the home seller gets to select the agent that they wish to retain and compensate, so do Buyers. In fact, this major change in how Buyers now compensate their Buyer Agents was recently and enthusiastically covered throughout the news. Because I will be representing you as your fiduciary, means that I possess an ethical responsibility to always place your needs first, over both the home seller and myself. Full Buyer Agency also means that I will be just as committed to showing you listings off the market, for sale by owner, new construction, etc., as I am regarding showing you conventional listings. I just want to ask you... would I have your permission to try to talk you out of a home you want if I believe that property was not in your best interest? Because that is also what full agency should mean. I would also like to share with you other ways that I view my agency and ethical obligations to my Buyer Clients. First, I'm not going to aks you for any privileged or financial information until or unless you ask me to represent you today, as that information could be used against you if I was representing somebody else and not you in a negotiation."

"I would also like you to know that just as Seller Agents use ChatGPT to describe a home in a way that the seller will receive more money in the sale, I use this tool to also ask for negatives about homes in towns, even though we know that no home is perfect (and we don't want to use that against ourselves) but it's a great negotiating tool... as my job is not to sell more homes when I represent Buyer, it's to sell more homes for less.
How does that sound?"

Every Buyer first asks themselves: Do they like the Buyer Agent? Can they trust the Buyer Agent? How do you establish trust in the first five minutes? Have you ever thought about it? A lot of thought went into this opening because you can't tell people you just met that "they can trust you" you have to provide them with a concrete and, perhaps, unexpected example of professional trust. By completely and surprisingly telling them that you cannot ask for financial information until you are representing them, establishes you with a level of trust similar to how ethical attorneys, doctors, and psychiatrists deal with issues of confidentiality and trust.

Access

"As your Buyer representative, I will also skillfully ensure you have access to all of the properties that you tell me fit your criteria, purchasing power, and interests. I possess what I believe is the best CRM in the entire real estate industry to serve you. The benefit of the technology I use is that you can visit my website and see essentially all of the properties on the market. Then my CRM will be able to alert you to all the properties that fit your interests by geography, type of home, price range, and all of the other criteria we discuss. The benefit to you, by relying upon my website and CRM, is that you will not have to do a generic search where your data and Buyer behavior will be auctioned or sold as a 'lead'. Coming to my website and letting my CRM alert you for properties you might be interested in will protect you from being relentlessly pursued by other agents. How does that sound?"

Arrange

"I am known in my company for my ability to get my Clients into the homes they need to see and, of course, as much as possible during the time when they need to see them. It is tragic how many Buyers miss out on opportunities simply because their agent could not arrange for timely showings. This unfortunate situation arises when a Buyer Agent is too busy prospecting for additional Sellers and Buyers, instead of putting their Buyer Client's needs above all others. In addition, I pledge to you, that if I have the privilege of representing you, I will do everything possible to arrange for appointments, including homes not listed, or taken off the market, if any of these properties you find to be either irresistible or of particular interest. I have established exceptional working relationships with most of the top Seller Agents in the market. I always get immediately back to them after all showings, make sure I turn off all the lights, and show respect for the Seller Agent in front of their Client. All of this helps to ensure that I am able to, very effectively, arrange for showings. Which is all the more important in the low inventory market we are in currently."

Apprise and Negotiate

"I will apprise you on every property you consider to discuss its value based upon my experiential knowledge of homes, streets, neighborhoods, school districts, style of homes, potential resale value, remodeling potential, and pricing. I will approach the evaluation of property value as if I were buying the home myself or you were a family member. My "appraisal and negotiating abilities" will also play a role in how I negotiate on your behalf. My negotiating philosophy, by the way, is that my Buyers should possess the greatest leverage in a negotiation..."

Apprise and Negotiate (cont.)

"...This is because there are many homes that you as a Buyer can purchase, and therefore can walk away from any sale. However, the home seller has only one property, which places more pressure on them. All I ask is that when I show you folks homes and we meet the Seller Agent, I don't care how much you love any home, please don't display excessive enthusiasm, or this could be perceived as a negotiating weakness 'tell'. Also, because I will be representing you, I will do something through the use of A.I. that no seller Agent will ever provide either us or their Client. Specifically, and in the spirit of full transparency, as mentioned earlier, I will prompt Chat GPT in the following ways: I will ask for a response that not only covers why someone should want to buy that particular home or move to that town but also why someone **should not buy that home or move to that town!** This way we will use A.I. to reveal concerns to the Seller Agent from an objective source as opposed to indelicately offending either the Seller Agent or their Client."

"Now, of course, we never would want to talk ourselves out of a great opportunity for you to buy the right home. Privately, I will be able to put into context both the good and bad of any home and town and do so with much more relevance than the imperfections delivered through A.I. I will also use Zillow's Zestimate within our negotiations when the estimate is in our favor. Regarding apprising you of property values, I will not only do a Buyer CMA (which will provide you with an estimate of value, as most Buyer Agents will) I will do something that others do not do... when you become very interested in a property and on the verge of buying the home, I will also do what I call an 'MMA'. A merchandising marketing analysis will also provide you with an estimate of what it might cost for you to significantly improve the value of that home through merchandising or remodeling. Many of my Clients have made tremendous profits through additional merchandizing, after buying the home, and I think that before someone buys a home they should be made aware of its potential. How does that sound to you folks?"

Apprise and Negotiate (cont.)

Editors Note: When I shared this concept with Martha Mosier (a CEO of a major CA brokerage) she said, "For my company, I want to take this idea and call it an RMA... a Resale Market Analysis!"   So, let me ask you this, reader: "Where do you believe you provide greater value? A Buyer CMA or a Buyer MMA... or Both?"

Administration

"Last year our brokerage administrated over _____ number of transactions. Essentially, we have made a science out of creating seamless transactions. I will be sharing the process a little later. I would also like to discuss with you, your potential mortgage and insurance needs."

Answers

"I am also committed to continually providing answers to any of your real estate lifestyle, mortgage, title, apprisal, etc. questions, and, to the degree possible, I will be responding promptly. Another way I will be answering any questions that you have about properties or communities will be through the videos and virtual tours I can conduct for you on homes or neighborhoods that you are not able to visit."

After the Sale

"Folks, the word 'after' stands for 'after the sale'. Most home Buyers live in their new home for an average of over ten years. I personally hope that you will be adding to our great community for at least the length of time. This means that you will probably encounter maintenance needs. Or you might want to do remodeling. Therefore, I will be presenting you with a directory of service providers. While we do not guarantee their work, I proudly recommend them for how they have demonstrated reliability and honorable results. By the way, one of my Clients told me that my Clients-only service directory was like having a five-year headstart living in the community."

After the Sale (Cont.)

"This comprehensive list of recommended tradespeople and service professionals will make your life a lot easier and less complicated. Also, just because you buy from me does not mean I say 'bye' after the sale. As I won't. You will never become a 'Past Client' of mine. Incidentally, if for any reason you decide to retain my services – and remember you don't pay anything if you do not buy a home from me – I will still be providing you today with my home service providers directory."

Here is my "homemade" video sample presentation

"Determine your personal 7 A's"

Before your Buyer Representational Value Presentation, and as part of your Buyer Consultation, how do you introduce the subject of
Buyer Compensated Representation?

My example was, "What would you expect from me as your Buyer Agent?

1. What is your opening?

2. How would you explain each of The 7 A's (me, lifestyle, financial, and all related answers to questions)?

AGENCY

How do you ask permission to ask questions throughout the process?

_____

_____

ACCESS

How would you explain how you provide Access to home information regarding both 'on' and 'off-market' properties?

_____

_____

ARRANGE

How do you explain your Value in Arranging appointments with properties, home inspectors, mortgage, etc. ?

_____

_____

APPRISE AND NEGOTIATE

How do you explain how you Apprise Buyer Clients of property values and how you NEGOTIATE on their behalf? What examples will you use of past negotiating successes?

_____

_____

_____

ANSWERS

How do you introduce the importance and value regarding your ability to provide trusted answers and advice?

_____

_____

_____

_____

ADMINISTRATE

How would you provide examples of your value regarding transition management?

_____

_____

_____

_____

AFTER THE SALE

How do you position your ongoing value and how you will never treat your present clients as 'past clients'?

_____

_____

_____

_____

Summary

Agency – your needs will always come first.

Access – you will have significant exposure to both available and non-available properties.

Arrange – I have spent years developing mutually respectful relationships with most of the top listing/marketing agents and I will also arrange appointments, if you like, with mortgage, insurance, title, (where relevant) attorneys, etc.

Apprise and Negotiate – I will be providing you with my expert knowledge on pricing, and property values, which will be critical in our negotiations.

Answers – I will be forever vigilant in -getting you the information you need.

Administration – I will be reviewing all the steps of the transaction.

After the sale, I will continue to serve you!   Do you have any questions?"

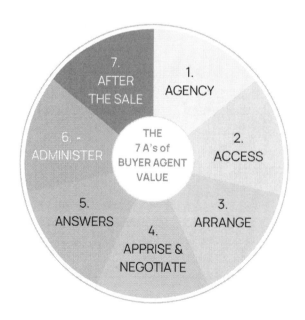

CLOSING THE AGREEMENT EXAMPLES

1

Agent: "Can you think of anything you would want from your Buyer representative, that I have not included?"

Buyer: "No, this is very impressive."

Agent: "Great, let's review the agreement."

2

Agent: "Folks, you said you wanted to be in your new home by the summer, therefore we have a little time pressure. So, when would you like to begin working together?"

Buyer: "As soon as possible."

Agent: "Well, I am ready if you are. So, let's get the paperwork out the way and get started."

3

Agent: "I know in your profession you are not used to doing work for someone without definitely getting paid. But that is how real estate works. So, I am going to ask you to retain me, even though you may never end up having to pay me."

4

Agent: "I am thrilled to have you as a new Client, let's get started."

5

Agent: "In your opinion, do you feel that I will be able to help you with all of your real estate needs?"

Buyer: "Absolutely."

Agent: "Great, then let's memorialize our relationship and review the paperwork."

CLOSING THE AGREEMENT EXAMPLES (cont.)

6

Agent: "Folks, 70% of Buyers only interview one agent before getting started. I hope that I am still in that 70% category, lol. Would you like me to represent you? And by the way, after we get you the right home and lifestyle, if you try to give me an additional bonus, please know that I cannot ethically accept one."

7

Agent: "Folks, I am one of the most successful agents in this market, as you would see if you checked my reviews and results. But I know that means nothing to you if we don't find you the right home. Right? So, let's get started, shall we?"

8

Agent: "I have a sense, because of the company you worked for and the impression that you make, that when I do a great job for you that you will become a great source of referrals. Yet finding the right home, and negotiating effectively for it, comes first. Are you ready to start working together?"

9

Agent: "Folks, there are a lot of questions I'd like to ask you about your motivation to buy, and how much you are willing to spend, that I didn't because I'm not comfortable asking questions until I am retained as your agent. This is because I don't believe an agent should ask for information that could in turn be used against the Buyer if I represent either a Seller or another Buyer you are either negotiating with or competing against."

Buyer: "I am an attorney and I must tell you how impressed I am with your ethics. In fact, I'm quite surprised. I now completely trust that you will only perform in our best interests."

GAINING TRUST IN A PRESENTATION

Research reveals that **trust** is based upon:

Knowledge – displays knowledge at the beginning of the process (ie. emailing, video, texts, etc.)

Communication/Clarity – Buyers do not make commitments when they are confused or when you are incoherent.

Compassion – Here is an example of a lack of compassion. A Buyer says they are moving because their mother died and the agent's body language is the same as if they had said, 'We had a flat tire driving here this morning."

Authenticity – People can spot affected behavior immediately... humor can be very helpful. As an example, when meeting home sellers of estates, I would say, "I grew up in a similar size home as this but unfortunately there were five other families living there."

Integrity – If you don't have an answer, say so, and never say something like, "Oh, this house is clearly going to go up in value."

THE FIVE C's OF EFFECTIVE PRESENTATIONS

1. Commitment
2. Confidence
3. Competence
4. Character
5. Caring

Always tell yourself that you are going to love the Buyers. They will feel this, they will reciprocate, and you will get the Buyer Agreement signed.

FIVE QUESTIONS EVERY BUYER ASKS THEMSELVES BEFORE SIGNING A BUYER AGREEMENT

1. Do I like the salesperson?
2. Do I trust the salesperson?
3. Is this a good decision?
4. Should I make this decision?
5. Should I make this decision now?

As you construct your Buyer Agreement Presentation, check to see if **all five elements are satisfied**.

QUESTIONS AND DISCUSSIONS

1) How do you prepare for every Buyer Presentation?

2) How much have you role-played, especially if you do not have a history of asking for compensation in your prior work with Buyers?

3) List the top 5 things you do for Buyers:

_____

_____

_____

_____

_____

4) Describe situations where you have negotiated effectively on behalf of Buyers so you can provide evidence.

_____

_____

_____

_____

5) When do you review your Buyer-side Agreement?

6) What is your strategy to convert unrepresented Buyers at open houses to Buyer Clients?

7) Do you think that you should offer a guarantee (one where you will perform certain activities or release Buyers from the contract)?

8) What if the Buyer says, "Someone else will represent us for less" How would you respond?

ADDITIONAL QUESTIONS TO BRING UP WITH Buyers

- How long have you been looking?

- What are the most important considerations in looking for your next home?

- What are your absolute musts?

- How would you rank the importance of the following: the neighborhood, the home itself, the schools, the style of home?

ADDITIONAL QUESTIONS TO BRING UP WITH Buyers (cont.)

- What is your price range... ballpark?

- Do you have to sell your home before you buy your next one?

- Would you like my assistance in helping you find a great lender?

- Would you be interested in buying a home that needed improvements?

- What is your timetable for moving?

- Would you consider paying less for a home if you thought it was a great investment but lacked some features?

- Would you consider paying more for a home if it was amazing to you?

- You have shared that you have interest in school information. We have provided a guide. Would you like me to email it to you?

- You told me that you bought homes in the past, what did you like the most about the agent who represented you? Was there anything about an agent that bothered you?

- What are your thoughts regarding when Buyers pay their own fee?

- Will this make you less enthusiastic about paying a referral fee?

- Will this make you less enthusiastic about accepting relo referrals?

Monitoring and Distributing Value

I often referenced, when I was CEO of Realtor.com, how 98 to 99% of site visitors clicked 'find a home' and only 1 to 2% clicked 'find a Realtor®'. This was because visitors to the site first wanted to evaluate homes which would then lead to a Buyer Agent .

I have a question that I would like to pose to all Buyer Agents, "Do you believe, as I do, that as more Buyers come to realize that they will now be expected to directly compensate the Buyer Agent they will also now become more likely to **also search and evaluate potential Buyer Agents**... and with more scrutiny?"

This is why I wish to highlight

I encourage you to contact Real Grader about how your use of social media rates with prospective Buyers and Sellers. You should learn how your use of social media to increase your **range, reach, and influence** as your number-one lead generation system is being viewed by prospective Clients! Real Grader can help you measure, manage, and maximize your digital presence, reputation, and perceived Value... which means more money, plain and simple. Check out their website.

MEASURE YOUR DIGITAL PRESENCE, ONLINE REPUTATION, AND BUYER SIDE VALUE

Buyers are looking you up on Google? Have you googled yourself lately?

The first impression of Buyer-Side Value is **online**. Prepare for the changing market.

REAL GRADER can help you improve your Buyer-Side Value online.

Would you like a **free audit** of your digital presence, online reputation, and Buyer-Side Value on these <u>eight sites</u>:

Google

Facebook

Instagram

LinkedIn

YouTube

Realtor

Zillow

Homes

It never hurts to check how consumers are perceiving your Buyer Agent Value, especially in this changing market. Check out their website today:

Most real estate professionals are familiar with the term 'S.E.O.' Which stands for 'Search Engine Optimization." It is very difficult for any company (never mind individual Agents) to come up on the top of a Google or other search engine page – organically or through paid search.

This is either because it is too expensive for paid placement or the complex algorithms that propel Google Bots do not wish to rank your content as high as you like...

This is why after seeing how **Chalk Digital** worked for real estate companies, I introduced a different meaning of SEO:

Seek Engine Optimization!

If you want to generate Buyer Leads without paying 'tariffs', then learn how Chalk Digital does – through their mobile-targeted geo-fencing reach out to open house Buyers, rental buildings, feeder markets, and Sellers who become Buyers. Check out their website.

Here is what Andrew Undem has to say about **BombBomb** video services:

"Buyer Agent Value can be best communicated to potential Buyer Clients before ever meeting them through Buyer-relevant videos. As important as the creation of your video content is, of greater importance is your means of distribution. BombBomb has redefined and perfected video content distribution. Here are some screenshots of how it has benefitted me across all platforms…"

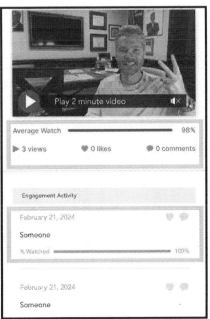

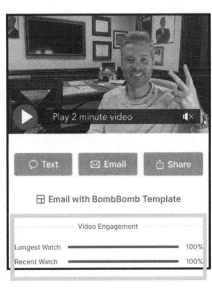

"Check out **BombBomb** for yourself and see how its targeted video services can help you, your team, or your company elevate your social media and overall online impact."

In my opinion, there is no individual in the real estate industry better equipped than **Jimmy Burgess** to speak to the critical subject of optimizing Buyer Agent Range, Reach, and Influence through the effective integration and **strategic use of video** and a range of social media marketing platforms.

Jimmy is a featured speaker, a valued contributor through the prestigious Inman News empire, and a highly respected mentor regarding Artificial Intelligence. If you have already subscribed to Jimmy's channel then forgive the obvious, if you have not, then do so or you will miss out on one of this book's greatest takeaways. **Buyer Agents could have no greater friend.**

Watch Jimmy's YouTube video:
'24 Ways to Generate Real Estate Leads in 2024'

- Do you plan to spend more time in the future representing Buyers or Sellers?

- Are you satisfied with your present Buyer Agreement Presentation?

- Do you believe there will be more advertising of fees than ever?

- How many people will you role-play your Buyer Agreement and Presentation with before you present it to potential Buyer Clients? Remember medical students first practice on cadavers!

I encourage you to visit the segment within this consulting report titled: The Cost to Buyers When Not Using an Agent. That process perhaps will enable you to deepen your resolve regarding your indispensable value.

SUMMARY

Buyer Agents are going to have to "productize" their Buying-side methodology in the same way they have done on the marketing side. One additional way of accomplishing this is, if you are willing to guarantee that you will provide the 7 A's of Buying-side Value, you might do so in the following fashion:

"The _____ (Company or Team) Buyer Value GuarAntee"
The 7A's of Buyer Agent Value... guaranteed!

or Buyer Agent Representational GuArantee!

Please first check with your attorney.

NOTES

SEMENT 2

A CASE STUDY OF
A WORLD-CLASS
BUYER AGENT

An interview with Julie Vanderblue
Fairfield County, Connecticut

62

A word about Julie Vanderblue:

Please meet Julie Vanderblue. As a former president and co-owner of a 60-office real estate brokerage and then the CEO of Reatlor.com, it's understandable that I would be both knowledgeable and selective when choosing the right Buyer Agent. When my family moved from California to Connecticut, I selected Julie Vanderblue. As you learn more about Julie, it will become apparent that my wife, Carol, and I made the right decision.

•••

DALTON: Julie, I want to begin by discussing something I know you never talk about and we've never discussed. A subject that I know that every single reader would be curious to know and for readers to get a sense of the level of success of the person who's providing them advice... how much personal volume over the last five years or so have you averaged?

JULIE: My personal productivity, which is exclusively 100% of my transactions, has ranged from 120 million to 150 million per year. At the same time, our great team produces between 200 and 280 million per year. I do however "touch" every single transaction. I "field train" my brokers, bring them along with me and get them involved. My greatest passion is my devotion to the skill and career development of my team members... with whom I am blessed to be associated.

DALTON: Thank you, Julie. What percentage of your personal volume comes from Buyers versus Sellers?

JULIE: It's almost 50/50.

DALTON: Julie, I've heard many coaches and top agents say that they don't have as much interest in "serving Buyers" as "home sellers". What led you to experience such a pronounced equilibrium in terms of a 50/50 balance between Buyers and Sellers?

JULIE: I believe our industry has been disproportionally focused on Sellers vs Buyers. I feel strongly that Buyers should demand and certainly deserve the highest level of skill, service, and care, now more than ever. It became a mission of mine to focus on consumer-centricity, educating our Buyers on not only what they need before and during the purchase of a home, but long after.

DALTON; How much of your success is because of how you "sell" Buyers versus how you "educate" Buyers?

JULIE: That's an easy question. It is 100% educating Buyers. I teach my team, and my team teaches me, that we aren't 'salespeople' we are 'educators'.

DALTON (laughing): Careful! "Educators" aren't supposed to make as much money as you do.

JULIE (laughing): Well, it's not 'all about the money'. Money follows value and results when one provides strong skill sets, service, and communication... all of which are imperative. Regrettably, many Buyers Agents, and hopefully this will change now with the new approaches to Buyer compensation, don't provide the proper level of value regarding all of the many components within a buying process that I can proudly say my team does.

DALTON: Julie, you live in Fairfield County, and, typical of most suburbs along the East Coast, the county is sprinkled with individual towns and hamlets. How do you help Buyers narrow down their particular town? Please describe that process.

JULIE: It's really about listening and getting to know your Buyer and understanding their communication style. When you first talk to them you need to understanding 'how they will hear you'. But first, we listen. I believe strongly that Buyer agents should truly understanding the nuances of each town and be engaged in the towns that they serve.

JULIE (CONT.): This is also why I have developed, with your help Allan and Ryan Ward's, numerous community videos. Also, while you often hear agents, even some on my team, say, "I'll go anywhere," the question is, "Is everywhere they're going a town or community they enjoy deep knowledge about?" Now, I can't keep my very ambitious associate from "going anywhere" but when I refer a Buyer, I make it a point to only refer a Buyer to a member of my team who lives and fully understands all of the nuances of that town. Quite honestly, in the marketing of homes, it's actually different. I don't think you need to use a "neighborhood expert" when marketing a home in a town. I actually think it's better to have someone who can cross-market other communities, to draw people in, and expand the reach of the property through their networking.

DALTON: So, when it comes to Buyers, you want to refer them to a person who understands the towns they serve? How do you assure yourself that your agent truly knows that town in the way that is necessary to educate a Buyer?

JULIE: That's simple, I'm constantly testing and asking my agents to educate me! I believe you need to devote a remarkable amount of time not only the town but also really get to know the Buyer. My team has developed a discovery survey that enables us, during the Buyer consultation, to learn about the Buyer's district needs. Only then do we begin introducing them to the communities, based upon our overviews, that are of interest. Allan, is it okay if I emphasize that we never try to talk any Buyer into anything... either a town or a home, because we are representing them... while, when we are representing a seller we are more persuasive.

DALTON: Julie, what percentage of your Buyers have you helped convert from their original intent of buying in a particular town where they end up buying another?

JULIE: I would say about 30%.

DALTON: That's a high percentage. Has that percentage grown as your team and their knowledge of towns has grown?

JULIE: Yes, it's grown as our geographic experts within the team have learned to cross-market.

DALTON: So, in other words, if a team doesn't have a broader range of representation, that can actually be to the detriment of the Buyer ending up in a town that they would have preferred?

JULIE: Yes, in fact, I found that several of my Clients (people relocating both from the States and internationally) didn't end up in a town they would have preferred, solely because they were never educated. In fact, most Buyer agents would rather not introduce other towns as it just makes more work for them. Their belief is that it's not in their best interest to introduce other towns as it leads to more work than keeping the Buyers where they are and just finding them a home. When I introduce Buyers to other towns, it's for the Buyer's best interest... and most agents simply don't do that. Most Buyer agents might respond to a Buyer asking for another town option like, "Oh, you want to see Fairfield too? Okay," versus, "Let me tell you about Fairfield and see if that might be a good fit!"

DALTON: Let me ask you, Julie, oftentimes people speak monolithically about 'consumers'. They use the word 'consumer' to describe everybody, but it doesn't. Within the word 'consumer; there's an infinite number of subsets. The same thing can be said of Buyers. The industry talks in terms of 'sellers' and 'Buyers' and overlooks the fact that within each definition, there's a wide range of variance in terms of individual needs. To that point, you, more than any real estate agent I have seen in 50 States, have provided distinct service for distinct markets. Let's start by going through some of the offerings, divisions, systems, and solutions you provide various segments to all different categories of Buyers and the reasons behind them.

JULIE: Absolutely. The first one that pops into my mind is our "Urban to Suburban Division" because it was so timely during Covid. We had so many people coming from New York who were moving to Connecticut. Although the "Urban to Suburban Division" existed prior to Covid, it really skyrocketed… and I learned from you, Allan, the only connection you have with the Buyer is through their concerns.

Again, that is why listening is so important and, with the amount of Buyer agency out there, I need to strategically to get the attention of different segments of the market to get them to hear me… versus, "I can find you a home!" "Urban to Suburban Division" was developed to let by Buyers understand our agents have been through the process before. They understand the nuances of moving from city life to country life. Since we've been repeatedly through the process, we can walk Buyers through it and explain this important transition. What might seem obvious to most is not obvious to everybody.

JULIE (CONT.): Also, it doesn't matter where the Buyer is coming from. I've heard it a million times, "We will target market for you!" What many Buyer agents don't understand is that it is important to change the messaging. They try to go to the geographic but they put the same message out there for every single occasion… because they think they're "geographically targeting."What they aren't getting is the need to create messaging that will appear to different demographics and systems.

DALTON: Julie, that is so genius because you're not only providing reasons "why" they should move but you're causing them to internalize "how" they'd rather live... whether during or after a pandemic. Now, let's now move on to your next solution for Buyers. What would that be?

JULIE: Divorce and Separation is a topic nobody really wants to talk about but if you target market, they'll call you directly. Through our program, they have a safe place to find out about the process from a real estate perspective... though "Divorce and Separation" is more for the sellers because we're representing both parties... and sellers become Buyers. If you don't understand the mentality of a seller, you'll never be able to negotiate effectively for your Buyer.

DALTON: Julie, you said that this is a subject no one wants to talk about... I'm sure that many attorneys would disagree. Because this book is Buyer AGENT BE AWARE, how does this division make Buyers more aware of Buyer agent value?

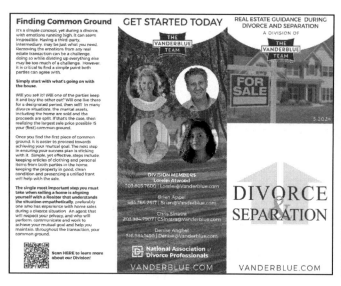

JULIE: With our Divorce and Separation Division we provide two agents on my team to communicate to and through this discussion. The result is that both parties feel completely represented. The benefit of this for a Buyer agent is that we've earned their trust by listening. Although it might not sound like a revelation, I can't stress enough that listening is the absolute key. When we sit down, even the divisions that are...

JULIE (CONT.): ...more focused on 'sellers', we are earning their trust when buying and for creating lasting relationships.

DALTON: Do you receive referrals from attorneys?

JULIE: Absolutely. Every single one of these divisions is an avenue to a conversation starter where we can prove our value to people for referrals... whether it's divorce attorneys or our Bridal division.

DALTON: What other division would you like to introduce to, I'm sure, a very appreciative reader?

JULIE: Move or Improve division! I learned that a lot of people coming to our open houses were considering renovating and simply looking to get design inspiration, so I devoted a division to this need. When someone at an open house says, "We're just getting ideas," I'd say, "Great! I'd love to chat with you about our Move or Improve Division. It could very well be that you should stay where you are... but I'd love to help you better understand the approximate value of your property as it is, the evaluation of your property value, and the actual cost of the renovation that you're going to do... and I have a litany of vetted professionals that can help you with the renovation if you don't have those... as well as evaluating what the property will sell for after the improvements when you're done. By helping them understand values before and after, they see that we can help create profit centers when they sell in the future vs overbuilding in areas that will not hold the value. Sometimes my Clients choose to 'overbuild', according to the financial spreadsheet, depending on the lifestyle they want to create, but they always appreciate the education. If they do stay where they are and improve, they usually use my network, which strengthens my relationships with our AIRE partners.... AND they talk about how great we are to their friends which leads to referrals. Through the Move or Improve program you'll really learn whether to buy or sell, with the absolute most amount of information and certainty, in order to make the right choices.

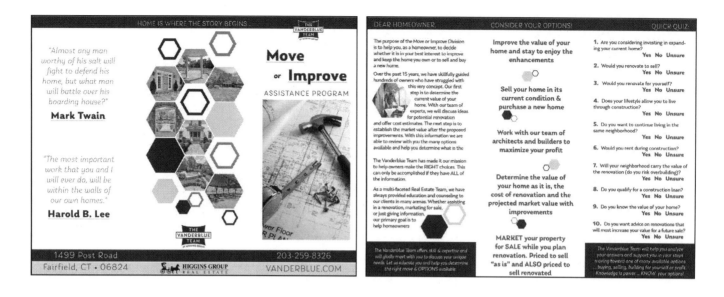

DALTON: Do you have a program for First-Time Buyers?

JULIE: Not just a program. We have a First Time Home Buyer Division.

DALTON: Wow, Julie, in an industry where many real estate professionals merely have a program for First-Time Buyers, and don't have the gravitas behind it, you actually have a division for first-time Buyers! When first-time Buyers learn you have a division just for them and their needs, how do they typically respond?

JULIE: With complete surprise and enthusiasm, Allan... and they say, "You actually have a Division for first-time Buyers" Speaking of my division, the only agents that I approve to represent this division are agents that have proven that they possess the proper temperament and patience. First-time Buyer require a different level of care, education, concern, and empathy...and sometimes those qualities do not coincide with our most energized, aggressive, and at times impatient associates. Although I wouldn't trade that category of associate for anything and deeply respect their work ethic.

DALTON: So you need somebody with the right temperament?

JULIE: Not just the right temperament but also the right skill set and knowledge. Each one of our divisions is led by a group and has a board member of the division. They meet on a monthly basis to discuss the next steps and where they're going. They 'round table' to create more value regarding that division and how to market it. Each one of these divisions is a tool for every single agent on the team to use.

DALTON: So if one of your team members meets with a home seller and ask, "What do you think is the most likely demographic coming to buy your home," and they respond, "People moving up," you can share that you have a division for that. What if they say, "Somebody Downsizing?"

JULIE: Well Allan, you do know we have a Downsizing with Distinction Division as well as 'Rightsizing' materials. Often if a home seller says, "I think the Buyers will come from New York," I explain that we of course we will target NY Buyers, in fact, we have an Urban to Suburban division to do just that. But we also target other Buyers with unique messaging through our other divisions. Downsizing with Distinction will appeal to Buyers moving from a larger home, Divorce and Separation Division will capture Buyers separating which is a very realistic potential Buyer for your home. I would name every division that we have that makes sense for their property, be it Senior Lifestyles, Relocation, InvestBlue, First-time home Buyers, or any of our others. This proves to them we have a strategic approach to not only get in front of a larger pool of real Buyers, but we have a system to influence them with specific messaging that attracts their attention.

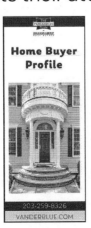

DALTON: How do you use your CRM to prospect and serve Buyers?

JULIE: We have tried countless CRMs over the decades I have been practicing Real Estate and, after much research, we concluded that Follow Up Boss is the best CRM for our team. It is the most user-friendly for TEAMS, allowing collaboration with agents so all involved are completely informed and nothing falls through the cracks. Agents can schedule, take notes, call directly from the CRM (whether on their phone or the computer), mass email with merge codes, create action plans, create video content to include in e-blasts or follow up (it syncs with Bomb Bomb which is what we use so that we can see exactly who opened and how long they stayed on the video and links we share, has a leader board that helps motivate and hold agents accountable...I could go on. It acts as a mini-assistant for agents as well as creates a road map for my own assistant and the ISAs who see all the leads as they come in or are added by agents. The proper CRM is imperative to nurture leads, keep in touch with partners, and communicate effectively with your Clients, staying in front of any problems that may occur rather than chasing solutions after the fact. The best CRM is the one you will actually implement, but I cannot stress enough the increase in ROI when it is used effectively.

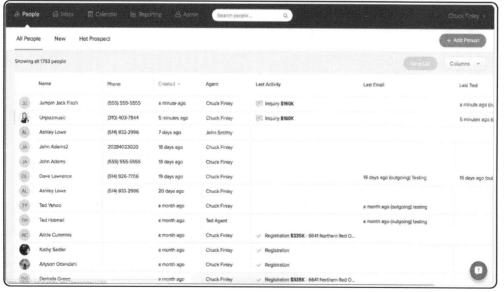

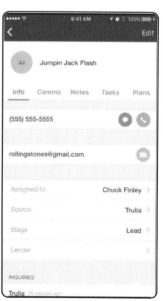

DALTON: Do you believe your CRM helps you secure more Buyers or more sellers?

JULIE: Sellers and we input Buyers. Sure, we input both but any lead gen system worth its salt will be dropped directly into your CRM. You can call them immediately and start your action plan in the shortest amount of time.

DALTON: Which lead gen systems are you using?

JULIE: Realtor.com, Zillow, Homes.com, GooglePPC, Google Local...

DALTON: Which is working best for you at this time?

JULIE: We pay Realtor.com for zip codes... and I have 28 mouths to feed... so we spend a lot of money on leads. Realtor.com is currently our most effective platform for our ROI. What I feel is most important about buying leads, and I'm talking about teams here, is teaching the agents how to fish and find their own leads... as I like to explain to them, "the lead gen we do is the frosting on the cake. The cake, in terms of joining The Vanderblue Team, is the education you'd get to cultivate your own referrals, your own leads, getting yourself out there, being a community expert, being in charge of a division, making a name for yourself. Making a brand for yourself within our team and, most of all, to help one another to learn and grow!

DALTON: As many will be reminded as they read this book, there's only one agent I have quoted consistently around the country over the years, and that is you, Julie. One of the major reasons is because of your epic innovation... Lifestyle Stories. Actually, the Lifestyle Story for the home we bought was the single major reason my wife and I bought our home in Fairfield when we were living in California. After you showed me the property, and then showed me the Lifestyle Story, I brought it back to California. When I unpacked, my wife took hold of it and then went...

DALTON (CONT.): ...to your video online. She became so deeply moved by what the previous homeowners had to say about the overall lifestyle of the home, that the next week I flew back and bought it... all because of the images and text in the Lifestyle Story.

JULIE: I remember that. I also remember you telling me that you didn't want to waste your time because you were planning on a move to Darien. Though, knowing you and Carol, I was certain you would value this unique property.

DALTON: Please talk about what the Lifestyle Stories are and how they help the Buyers.

JULIE: These beautifully created 10 to 15-page Lifestyle Stories are what truly differentiates our properties but it also creates a connection with the Buyers. Many might believe that they are only for the sellers because we do it in order to get the most amount of money for their property... but, as I learned from you, Allan, you need to fully utilize your Range, Reach, and Influence. The Lifestyle Stories create influence. They influence Buyers into making a decision to buy their home by cultivating an emotional Buyer. Every page has a purpose from the "photographic journey" and the story of the home, to the Top 10 things the seller loves about the home... which Zillow also started doing. Now, we didn't create Top 10s, maybe David Letterman did, but most Top 10s in regard to home sales are usually generic: "Oh, I love the kitchen because it has this, this, and this..." but the whole point of our Top 10s is to create an emotional connection with the Buyer so that they can visualize the lifestyle there. They're going to picture their own child sledding down that huge hill in the backyard. The benefit to the Buyers is that they get the whole story of the home to make a more comprehensive decision. They've been running in and out of houses. Typically, at the end of the day, they don't remember anything from those single page loose sheets of paper. With our properties, they go home with a thick book with fabulous content that will stay with them both physically and emotionally... just as it did with Carol, Allan.

JULIE (CONT.): Another important thing about the Lifestyle Stories is that, unlike 99% of the home information distributed by agents, they include all of the home's improvements and are up-to-date! One last thing regarding Lifestyle Stories... they also create new Buyers for us because they build trust in our new relationships. That's why we do 10 to 15 open houses every chance we get. It's your one opportunity to be in front of people as if they walked into your store... and they don't just walk out with a little two-sided sheet of paper!

DALTON: Julie, one last thing. You've created a concept that a lot of major brokerages and brands are predicated upon... and that's the extension of services and value that goes beyond the transaction to provide value before, during, and after the transaction. Unlike others though, you've instead created... what's it called?

JULIE: All Inclusive Real Estate... or AIRE. AIRE isn't actually a division of The Vanderblue Team, it's actually its own entity. Think of it more as a network. AIRE is a strategic way to create lifelong Clients because it includes something they will always need: the best of the best-vetted vendor and company relationships that my team and I have cultivated over the past 27 years. Where do people typically find these things now? You can't go to Google as most of those results are sponsored or pay-to-play... even many with fake reviews. My future and longtime Clients have AIRE and it is something they can trust. AIRE was also created as an online resource as all day, every day various Clients would call me to ask, "Hey, Julie! Do you happen to know... or do you have someone who...?" It is always flattering that they are coming to me and my team first, because of the trust we have developed, but AIRE being online has streamlined the process

DALTON: Genius, Julie! Thank you so much for sharing everything you and your team are doing for your Buyer Clients.

JULIE: It's been a pleasure, Allan!

JULIE (CONT.): Another important thing about the Lifestyle Stories is that, unlike 99% of the home information distributed by agents, they include all of the home's improvements and are up-to-date! One last thing regarding Lifestyle Stories... they also create new Buyers for us because they build trust in our new relationships. That's why we do 10 to 15 open houses every chance we get. It's your one opportunity to be in front of people as if they walked into your store... and they don't just walk out with a little two-sided sheet of paper!

DALTON: Julie, one last thing. You've created a concept that a lot of major brokerages and brands are predicated upon... and that's the extension of services and value that goes beyond the transaction to provide value before, during, and after the transaction. Unlike others though, you've instead created... what's it called?

JULIE: All Inclusive Real Estate... or AIRE. AIRE isn't actually a division of The Vanderblue Team, it's an entity all it's own. Think of it more as a network. AIRE is a strategic way to create lifelong Clients because it includes something they will always need: the best of the best-vetted vendor and company relationships that my team and I have cultivated over the past 27 years. Where do people typically find these things now? You can't go to Google... as most of those results are sponsored or pay-to-play. Even worse, many have fake reviews!

JULIE (CONT.): My future and longtime Clients have AIRE and it is something they can trust. AIRE was also created as an online resource as all day, every day various Clients would call me to ask, "Hey, Julie! Do you happen to know… or do you have someone who…?" It is always flattering that they are coming to me and my team first, because of the trust we have developed, but AIRE being online has streamlined the process

DALTON: Genius, Julie! Thank you so much for sharing everything you and your team are doing for your Buyer Clients.

JULIE: It's been a pleasure, Allan!

Julie Vanderblue would love to be an extension of your professionalism when referring all those buying or selling in Fairfield County. Feel free to connect with Julie at **julie@vanderblue.com**

SEGMENT 3

A LUXURY LEGEND

An interview with Cristal Clarke
BHHS Global Network's #1 Producing
Luxury Specialist

CRISTAL CLARKE WAS HONORED AT THE 2O24 BERKSHIRE HATHAWAY HOMESERVICES CONVENTION AS THE NUMBER ONE PRODUCING AGENT IN THE ENTIRE GLOBAL NETWORK FOR THE FOURTH CONSECUTIVE YEAR!

DALTON

Cristal, I've heard innumerable top-producing real estate agents declare, "I don't want to spend too much time with buyers!" Is this your attitude?

CRISTAL

No, Allan. I similarly hear people say, "I don't want to deal with renters." My philosophy is that Renters can possibly turn into Buyers and Buyers, if you provide the service they expect, can ultimately turn into Sellers at some point and become repeat clients. In my opinion, Buyers are just as important as Sellers – you simply have to set ground rules for expectation levels at the start. If they do not agree, then maybe they are not real Buyers anyway. If I am spending my time and effort, I expect the same commitment in return.

DALTON

Although you are the number-producing agent, among approximately fifty thousand worldwide, you have never developed a team that included any or several buyer agents. Why not?

CRISTAL

The reason is, Allan, if a client(s) calls and wants to hire me – and the knowledge and service level that I bring to the table – for me to say to that potential client or even an existing client, "Oh, here is X who works with me!" In my opinion, that says to the client that I do not have time to deal with them ... even though they took the time to call me.

If that were me, I would be moving on to someone who does have the time to speak with me and not push me off to their assistant. This is a service industry and clients expect service.

DALTON

I suspect this is a question you have never been asked before but here goes... What has been more impressive to you, the luxury properties you have marketed and sold or the sellers and buyers of these properties?

CRISTAL

Properties come and go. Clients, in many instances, turn into friends and that relationship is more cherished than a single piece of real estate or a transaction. Don't get me wrong, I have represented some amazing properties ... but I value the experience of the relationship above all else.

DALTON

What are some keys to working with high and ultra-high-net-worth buyers?

CRISTAL

Treat them with appreciation but as an equal. If you can not talk to them on the same level that they do business you will not be doing business with them. If they have called you it is for a reason, so be positive, confident, and appreciative of the opportunity but do not appear like they are doing you a favor. In many instances, the roles can be reversed in that regard.

DALTON

What is the key to working with their representatives or entourages?

CRISTAL

Accept their position in the transaction and do not, under any circumstances, try to leave them out in any way. They are in place for a reason as a trusted employee or representative of the client. Do not question that and embrace the opportunity to solve issues without involving the client. They have in-depth and inside knowledge that you do not have.

DALTON

What do you attribute your epic success in working with luxury buyers to?

CRISTAL

At the end of the day, Buyers are Buyers just like people are people. Everyone is different in their own way so you have to adapt to individual nuances and not try to make everything generic. Just because something worked for one client does not mean it will work for every client. Most importantly, be confident and enthusiastic about the opportunity you are being given. If the opportunity provides itself, take time to talk about things other than the transaction. Research your client, find out their likes and dislikes, make them feel comfortable that you have their best interests at heart and are not just there for the deal.

DALTON

Do you find it easier or more difficult to negotiate on behalf of the ultra-rich versus those who are merely affluent?

CRISTAL

Sometimes, yes. The more people can spend the more idiosyncrasies they may have. As an example, I had one transaction that did not come to a conclusion because the Buyer wanted a statuary piece in the garden and the Seller would not let it go ... so it became a case of "I want" versus "you can not have." Also, ultra-rich Buyers tend to compromise less because they do not have to and they can pay for the property that fits all their wish list items not just some of them ... maybe they want a different size or shaped pool or the tennis court in a different location.

DALTON
What are some of the things that turn luxury buyers off the most?

CRISTAL
Being perceived as uneducated and that they can be taken advantage of. Just because they can afford something does not mean they will overpay for something. They didn't get where they are without some great sense of business acumen.

DALTON
Do you find that the ultra-rich want more to buy a property that is visible to admirers or one more private and sequestered?

CRISTAL
I think that depends on the client and also on the market location. Los Angeles for example can attract Buyers who like to have trophy properties which telegraph, "I have arrived." Other areas such as Montecito and Santa Barbara tend to attract Buyers who want to be a little less conspicuous and stay away from the limelight. That's not to say only Los Angeles and Montecito attract a certain type of Buyer but I think it's all personal preference and based on their lifestyle at a given moment and may include business and family considerations.

DALTON
Has your brand helped you with Luxury buyers and which aspects of the brand's marketing resources do you use the most?

CRISTAL
When I mention our brand, certain things come to mind such as stability, permanence, presence, and trust. When dealing with luxury real estate and luxury Buyers the last thing they want is drama. In all likelihood, they have many business commitments and time is limited.

CRISTAL (cont.)

They want a company and an agent who can bring calm to the storm if there is a storm ... and we all know things happen in a transaction. They also want reassurance that the decisions they are making are valid and based on solid information and data. What other company is there that brings all this under one umbrella? This is the reason I am with BHHS. If you want to be the best you need to associate and surround yourself with the best.

DALTON

Do you believe you enjoy equal value with buyers or sellers?

CRISTAL

Yes, each is rewarding in their own way and for different reasons. For Sellers, it is seeing the realization of their dream come to fruition and all the work that went into creating a home realizing and exceeding their expectations when it sells. For Buyers, it is making that call to tell them that their offer was accepted and hearing the joy in their voice and the thankfulness that they have for making their dream come true.

DALTON

If we see the day when most, if not all, buyers will be asked to pay buying-side fees, how confident are you that you will be able to command fees equal to what buyer-side agents are paid by the seller, especially given our price points?

CRISTAL

I see no reason for fees to be diminished to a great extent. A buyer pays to have the representation that they expect and either that is paid by a Seller and included in the price of the real estate or the price of the real estate is reduced to account for additional Buyer costs/fees.

DALTON

What are your three most important skills when representing buyers?

CRISTAL

In-depth knowledge of the market. Confidence in the advice being given and that it is unbiased to ensure the client's decision-making process is the right one for them at the right time … and not just so an agent can secure a commission. Negotiate, negotiate, negotiate.

DALTON

What type of data do you provide Buyers?

CRISTAL

We provide real-time data on what has sold and what is available on the open market, as well as off-market opportunities. We educate the Buyer as to the local area and different aspects within a defined demographic that they may be considering … which includes social amenities, schools, recreational aspects, and walkability … as well as discuss the pros and cons of each aspect of a potential acquisition, including financial aspects relating to the transaction and associated costs.

DALTON

Do you do many open houses for Buyers? Are you physically present?

CRISTAL

I think you mean open houses for Sellers? Yes, I do open houses for clients. As I mentioned earlier, when taking a listing a client is retaining my services based on my knowledge of the market and the expectation is that I will be there to represent the property to the best of my ability and impart my knowledge to any potential Buyer that may visit the property.

CRISTAL (cont.)

This gives me the opportunity to meet potential new clients or if the subject property does not work for them apprise them of other market opportunities that may fit their needs. It also gives me insight into how the property is being perceived by Buyers and if any adjustments may be needed in the presentation.

DALTON

Why do you never boast, especially, about your famous clients?

CRISTAL

Clients appreciate the confidentiality that I bring to all my transactions not just celebrity clients. As with any transaction, there are pitfalls and hurdles to cross, and clients need to feel comfortable in the knowledge that talking about items that may be contentious at times and that what are meant to be private discussions between the client and their agent will not be at some late point tabloid fodder. The old saying of "loose lips can sink ships" could easily be amended to "loose lips can ruin a career in real estate!"

DALTON

Do you find it necessary to sell Santa Barbara or does it sell itself?

CRISTAL

Many people come to Santa Barbara and Montecito knowing ahead of time what the area has to offer: great climate, a wonderful school system, indoor/outdoor living, and a more reserved sense of self. So, no, I do not necessarily feel the need to sell our local communities, rather, I highlight the areas that may be of special interest to that particular client.

DALTON
Do you have a method of helping your buyers navigate multiple offers?

CRISTAL
Multiple offers can be an agent's worst nightmare. If not handled correctly, you run the risk of losing all of the potential Buyers. My advice to clients is, generally, let's take the "best" offer. This is not specifically based on price but a multitude of factors of which price is just one element. The overall terms should be what's looked at. If that one offer comes together then run with it to closing, or if it falls out, look to the backup offer. I generally find agents who have missed out on behalf of a client – if you are upfront with them and explain it was a case of better terms, not price – they will be more receptive and advise their clients to go for that backup position.

DALTON
Do you market yourself more for listings or buyers?

CRISTAL
My position is that I sell real estate, whether that be representing a Buyer or Seller, my representation is the same.

DALTON
How much does your prodigious commitment to charities influence celebrity clients if they meet you through charity work?

CRISTAL
I don't have an answer to this other than that contributions made are not done so with the intent to solicit the client. Rather it is done to help support the community that I call home and allows me to do what I do.

DALTON

Luxury Buyers are all individuals but if you had to say what are the top things you believe they value the most when buying property?

CRISTAL

- Honesty

- Knowledge of the marketplace

- Understanding their needs

- Patience in finding the right property, not just "a" property

- Placing their needs first

- Negotiating the best deal possible for them and then allowing them to feel comfortable walking away if it does not work...

- Knowing we will find "the house"

DALTON

Knowing what you now know, what would you do differently than you did if you were starting your career over?

CRISTAL

This is a difficult question to answer because what I did up to this point in my career has led me to where I am today and I am grateful for the position I am currently in. If changing anything I did previously would have taken me down a different road, given the choice, I would have stayed the course I took. In retrospect, I should have joined my present company earlier than I did but I believe there is a reason I did not and I am happy for the decisions I made when I made them. As they say, "all roads lead home" and I feel I am now home.

DALTON

Do luxury buyers look at more or fewer homes than average-price buyers?

CRISTAL

Luxury Buyers generally tend to have a very specific set of haves and needs in real estate and because of this, there are fewer homes that meet their pre-established criteria. As noted earlier, Luxury Buyers tend to make fewer compromises when buying real estate. They know what they want and what they don't want. A Buyer at a lower price point may be more flexible in their choices and also have more choices available.

DALTON

I know you are building another significant home in Santa Barbara are you more or less demanding than your community contemporaries?

CRISTAL

I feel we are more demanding but that is also our personality. We do not compromise in business and we do not compromise in the investment we make in real estate. Our philosophy is that if you are going to do something do it right and do it right the first time. Be committed and don't look back. The future is not behind you it is in front of you. Embrace it as you should embrace life!

DALTON

Thank you so much for all this, Cristal!

CRISTAL

You are more than welcome, Allan!

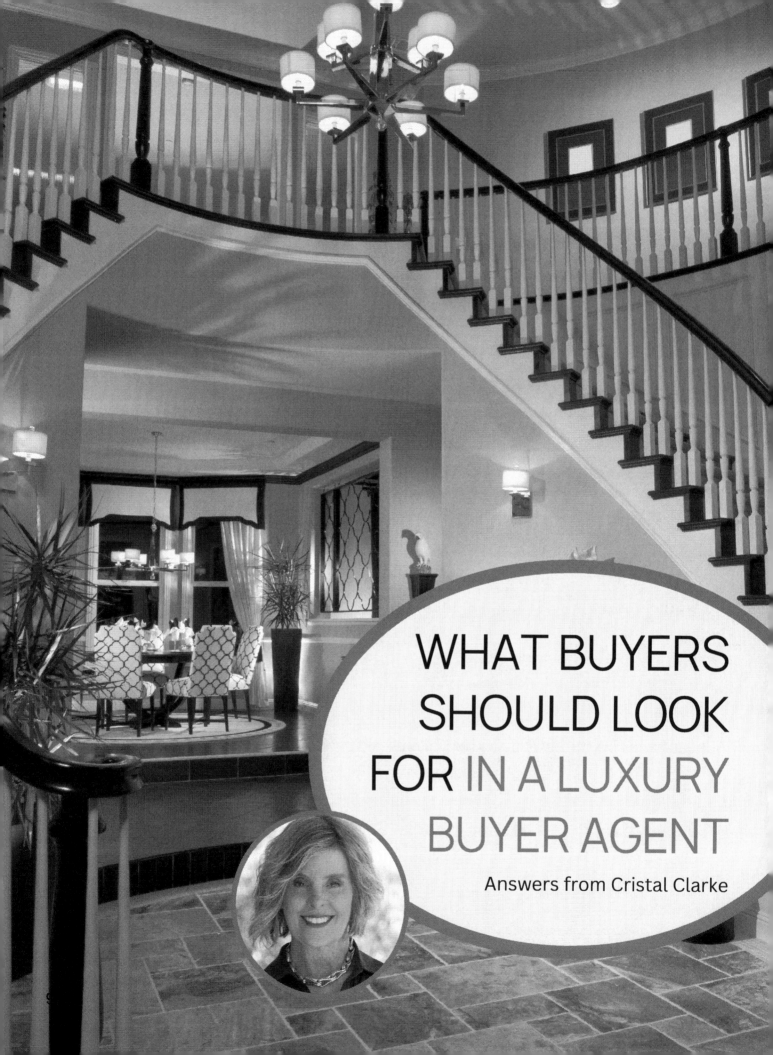

WHAT BUYERS SHOULD LOOK FOR IN A LUXURY BUYER AGENT

Answers from Cristal Clarke

I also asked Cristal to provide Buyer Agents her perspective on what a Luxury Buyer should look for in a Buyer Agent, in case Buyer Agents consider developing a brochure or posting content on social media... as her answers may stimulate how they go about addressing the subject.

What should Buyers look for in a Luxury Buyer Agent?

As with any relationship, and a Buyer Agent Agreement is a relationship, they must start from a point of trust. The Client, or potential Client, is entrusting you, or will be entrusting you, to advise them on an investment in real estate which, in all likelihood, will be the most significant investment in their lifetime... either in monetary outlay or a combination of cash and loans. In either scenario, they will be imparting significant amounts of funds and or taking on a significant amount pf debt. As such the advice you impart as a Buyer Agent will be the basis for their decision and one they will need to trust.

So how do you gain and warrant trust?

Firstly, you should have an in-depth knowledge of the marketplace in which you conduct business. Know, not only the current and past/sold inventory, but be familiar with and be prepared to talk about the areas of interest Buyers are seeking to purchase in. Be prepared to talk about the properties that have transacted within those areas, be it neighborhoods or within defined financial parameters. Talk about what the community has to offer in terms of amenities and other resources.

Second, Sit down with the Client, or potential Client, and outline their goals. Think of this as a Client giving you top ten list of things they would like in a property. This may be a property that has to have a specific layout, a certain number of bedrooms or configuration, if the Buyer has children does the bedrooms need to be on the same level or close to the primary bedroom, does the house have to be single level, has to have a pool or views, be close to schools. Whatever the preferences may be priorities those and this will give you the ability to focus the property search so as to not waste a Client's time.

Do not promise what cannot be delivered. Make sure the Client's expectation level is tempered so as to align with the market. If a Client is seeking, as an example, a 5-bedroom house with the primary bedroom on the same level as 3 other bedrooms and a 5th bedroom separate for guests with a pool and views in a specific neighborhood at a maximum price. Based on your knowledge of the market, if this is unrealistic you have a responsibility to be forthright with the Client from day 1. If you say no problem and cannot deliver options, the Client will start to second guess your ability. In short, manage your Client's expectations so as to install confidence and not foster uncertainty in your abilities.

What do Luxury Buyers care about most?

In my experience, Buyers care most about your integrity. A Luxury Buyer, or any Buyer, wants to know you have their best interests front and center and will not compromise just for a commission. You have to be willing to tell a Buyer that it's OK to walk away from a transaction.

Remember you have spent years creating a business, a career, and a reputation. Do not jeopardize it for one commission. Having the time to devote to them and provide the service they require. You were contacted because a Buyer, in today's real estate environment, has researched the marketplace they are potentially interested in and, based on that research, made a call to you and probably two of their agents. They want to know you have the time to devote to them as their time is valuable and possibly limited.

That you have an in-depth knowledge of the marketplace. Today's Buyers are real estate savvy. They probably know at least as much about the marketplace and the properties within it as you do and, in some cases, probably more. Buyers today research ahead of time and are property-specific in their needs. Today, a Luxury Buyer has many time constraints which may be based on business commitments, family life requirements, travel or just living life. They want an agent who can provide focused real estate options in a timely and efficient manner. If you waste a Client's time you will not have a Client for an extended period of time. Listen and ask. The Luxury Buyer of today will, in most cases, give you detailed information about what they require in a real estate purchase. Remember they will have already done their research and want to know you are up to the task. If they do not tell you what they want you should ask. Be prepared to be tested. They will want to make sure you are not intimidated and are prepared to ask meaningful questions so as to make sure your focus is on their needs.

What are your tips regarding what Luxury Buyers should look for when hiring their Buyer Agent?

Buyers first and foremost, in the luxury market and any market segment, should look for an agent that has the ability to **treat their Client as a partner.** The experience of buying real estate in the world we live in today is often filled with complex challenges and can be, if not handled correctly, stressful for a Buyer – Agent relationship.

An agent should present a sense of calm. When everything else around may be in a state of turmoil, a Buyer will want to know you have the skill set to handle situations that may arise in a transaction that were not anticipated... and as we all know, these arise more often than not!

A Buyer-Agent relationship is more than just about real estate. Buyers Agents should not only talk about real estate but also about the **community you live in or are conducting business in**. Buyers should look for agents who are community-focused, up-to-date on local events, interested in what the Client's interests are outside of real estate, and be able to focus conversations on areas of common ground. A Client wants to know you are not just there to close a transaction but rather welcome them into a community you are proud to live in and be a part of. Buyers should interview agents who have a fully-rounded...

...knowledge base about the community in which they are seeking to invest in and acquire real estate. Many communities have niche market segments and cultural and economic benefits that may not be apparent at first glance so you want an agent who can provide you with an in-depth overview of where you are considering to reside.

What top questions would you ask if selecting a Luxury Buyer Agent?

What is your level of expertise in representing Luxury Buyers in this marketplace?

Have you represented other Buyers in the price range I'm interested in?

Why should I choose you to represent me?

I notice you work alone and not as a team. Will you have enough time to devote to finding me the right property?

What are your working relationships with other agents and other companies?

Are you able to find and access off-market properties?

Should you have any additional questions regarding serving Luxury Buyers and Sellers, free to connect with Cristal at Cristal@Montecito-Estate.com

SEGMENT 4

EDU-Selling BUYERS

"Great salespeople are relationship builders who provide value and help their customers win."
— **Jeffrey Gitomer**

Real estate professionals, in order to succeed, need to develop several so-called core competencies. Marketing, merchandising, social media marketing, negotiating, and Selling. Forty or fifty years ago selling skills alone were the only requisite for success. It was listed as first among all necessary talents in real estate. Well in 2024/2025 and beyond, selling professionalism will re-emerge and reach a level of significance that has not been seen in decades. This is because it is generally accepted that when a real estate professional is representing a home seller they are in a marketing mode yet while working with Buyers a selling one.

Given how Buyer Agents increasingly will have to better define their value, in order to be directly compensated by Buyer Clients, will mean that buying side value and skills will attract more education, coaching, and overall attention. The challenge facing all real estate brokerages and professionals will be in how they define what it means to be a real estate salesperson ... as simple as such a definition might appear to some. Clearly, Buyer Clients when assessing the sales ability of their prospective Buyer sales Agent, will not be pondering the following :

"I hope this Agent will do a great job of selling us!"

Of Course Not!

Rather consideration surrounding ... how knowledgeable, how trustworthy, how skillful a negotiator, and how successful and likable the prospective Buyer Agent appears will be resoundingly more relevant to increasingly discerning Buyers contemplating to whom and how much will they will pay a Buyer Agent.

Issues of trust, knowledge, and professional skill therefore must be the qualities that comprise any new-age definition of a real estate salesperson or on this case a Buyer Agent.

What this means is that many of the approaches to selling must be summarily purged by real estate professionals.

Let us list some of the more prevalent approaches to selling and examine whether they should be a part of the career of a real estate salesperson moving forward.

The ABC Selling Approach

Alec Baldwin, in his epic presentation to the sales team at Mitch and Murray in the movie *Glengarry Glen Ross*, wrote the three letters ABC on the board, standing for 'Always Be Closing'. His extolling of those three words was purposeful. Those salespeople in the movie who were being harangued by Baldwin were provided leads of people (prospects and suspects) presumably interested in buying one singular product. That one product was the proverbial (at that time) Land for Sale in Florida. What was for sale therefore was one product, one decision with an hour to decide ... and one size fits all.

Not that the tone of Baldwin's 'coaching' should ever be normalized, one must admit (putting behavioral norms aside) that those techniques not only worked in that environment but enabled him to wear that finely tailored suit, expensive watch, and the sports car he had parked outside.

The ABC style of selling is absurd, completely inappropriate, and ineffective in real estate sales ... and even more so with Buyers over a protracted relationship. The reason is that anybody who is "always closing" is unlikely to ever provide the proper education, necessary information, and relationship-building trust that is indispensable in real estate sales.

The "Say Yes" Sales Technique

The "Say Yes" technique is laughably simplistic, and depending upon the degree of sophistication, insulting to those being abused. While some manipulative real estate speakers will ritualistically manipulate weak-minded audiences by encouraging them to yell out yes after making common sense declarations this approach should never be considered as transferable when engaged with "equals" during a real estate consultative process.

Can you ever imagine telling a Buyer the following :

"This is the perfect school system for your children. Say yes!"
"You'll never have a better agent than me. Say yes!"
"If you don't buy this house today it'll be gone tomorrow. Say yes!"

The F.A.B. (Featured Advantage Benefit) Selling Technique

Feature advantage benefit selling works well for when one is selling a product yet in real estate one must first sell a relationship and the sales consultant's own value before ever getting to a product. That said, FAB can be helpful in organizing mini-presentations … although it is not expansive enough behaviorally to serve as a comprehensive method of interaction throughout a protractive and advisory-based professional selling process.

Here's how it can be used: "I have been in real estate for twenty years and the advantage I have over most agents is that I have gotten to know the best way to negotiate with many agents in the market and the benefit to you will be that I usually can guarantee my Clients a most favorable result because of the trust I have developed with other agents."

FAB as a feature advantage benefit with evidence:

"Folks, I have sold over fifty homes in this market in the past two years. The advantage to you is that I possess a deep knowledge of competitive value and the benefit is that it will help us in any home I negotiate for my Clients. Let me show you some examples."

CONSULTATIVE SELLING

This is when the salesperson, as a "solutionist", first through appropriate questions determines the wants and needs of their Client and then prescribes solutions. This is a part of "new age real estate" and consistent with the role of a real estate trusted advisor but this methodology does not go far enough.

EDU-SELLING

The integration of education and selling best describes the most valuable selling role and behavior of a real estate professional. Edu-selling is solving problems and challenges in which proper decisions require being educated on the subject matter. One can not be a Real Estate Trusted Advisor without first becoming a gatherer of information ... and at the very least knowing how to access and interpret relevant information and data.

Because the real estate home buying process is more protracted and relational versus a marketing presentation to sellers, which is more of an event or an epic episode, it requires a more sustained face-to-face need to educate Clients ... especially when working with and for Buyers. This is because the buying process is different than a winner-take-all listing presentation where a real estate agent essentially has one shot and must place more emphasis on their merits. The Buyer process means that Agents have a longer time to get to know and adapt to the needs, in many cases, two Buyers, and be consistently responsive educationally.

"My" Take on Profiling Buyers

I deeply respect the accuracy of personality tests provided (there actually is a test taken). Where I encourage caution is when the brilliance of these tests is misappropriated and can actually result in counterproductive results in one's attempt to better understand and thus serve Buyers.

This means that personality profiling through programs like Disc or Myers Briggs used or misused in an attempt to pigeonhole consumers into one of four personality types in the case of Disc or eight behavioral tendencies in the case of BMI testing (Myers Briggs) should give way to not drawing such immediate conclusions. I suggest that instead a greater effort be expended, especially given the greater amount of time spent with Buyers than sellers in order to truly get to know the desires and how to best communicate with each individual. Remember these tests are classified as self-examination testing and they are very accurate, again when one actually takes the test ... that is the whole idea.

Now that we have examined various selling styles and when personality profiling is appropriate (and when it is attempted as a blatant and amateurish shortcut), let's now examine a communication model that will help guarantee that honest and open communication is achieved between you and each absolutely individual Buyer Client.

1) Don't ask Buyers for their loyalty, thank them in advance for loyalty (after all they have decided to meet with you). Although Buyer contracts might make this point somewhat moot for anyone who ever brings up loyalty with Buyers it is recommended that you **"thank" versus "ask" for loyalty.** Asking is about you ... thanking is about them.

2) Consider replacing business cards that read: "The sincerest compliment someone can pay me is to give me referrals of their friends and families" with "My greatest professional privilege is to serve the real estate needs of you, your family, and your friends."

3) Do not talk about qualifying the Buyer. Instead, speak of "establishing purchasing power". One is disempowering, the other is empowering.

4) Refine the inventory of available homes by professional probing, and displaying a knowledge of the market that helps to almost automatically dismiss choices that are either illogical or unattainable. "Based on what you are describing, there are approximately four homes that fit that description ... and I believe that all four are available ... for now."

5) "If we find what you are looking for what is your timetable to buy?"
    This is a nicer way to determine the sense of urgency.

6) Review Buyer Guarantee if you have one.

Communication model (after showing first home)

1) "Based upon what you have seen thus far, in your opinion does this home meet your family's needs?"

Purpose: The reason behind asking for opinions and a trial close is that opinions can be changed. This is a non-intrusive communication technique.

2) If the answer is, "No."

"Apparently, you have some reason for feeling this way may I ask what it is?"

Purpose: This response allows you to professionally meet the objection rather than trying to *overcome the objection* which you cannot. What you want to do is to learn what is the real concern or objection.

3) After concern is shared ...

"If you were not concerned with _____ then, in your opinion, do you think this home would fit your needs?"

Purpose: You must verify objections so you are responding to reasons and not excuses ... but you must do so in a respectful manner.

4) If the answer is, "Yes."

"That you think the bedrooms are too small may be the very reason why this might be a great opportunity." (This is called the reversal technique). "Do you like everything else about the home?"

If the answer is, "Yes."
Then... "If you had all of this and larger bedrooms it would cost another one hundred thousand."

Then there are numerous other things to say but this technique allows you to reverse objections as sometimes the reasons against something can also become the reasons for something.

Example: "I don't want to sign up for coaching because my schedule is too crazy." The fact that your schedule is so crazy is the very reason why you need coaching!

Another Example:

Buyers: "Well, thanks for showing us this very nice home."
    But they say nothing more.

Agent: "Well, based on what you have seen thus far, does this home meet your family's needs?"

Buyers: "Yes. It is very impressive!"

Agents: "Great! I thought you would be very impressed given everything you shared with me. Would you like to see if we can take this home off the market for you?"

Buyers: "Well, we're not ready to get that serious."

Agent: "Apparently, you have some reason for feeling that way."

Buyers: "We love the house but not the school system."

Agent: "If you were not concerned with the school system, even though many families love this school and they have numerous students who go on to elite universities, would you be interested in this home?"

Buyer: "I don't think we would move forward even if we loved the school."

Agent: "May I ask why?"

Buyers: "We think we're going to be waiting till next year anyway because we think prices are going to come down."

Agent: "Well no one can predict that and we are not allowed to ... but let me ask you this ... the home is on the market for 750 thousand. Worst case scenario, what do you think it would come down to by next year? Many people are saying that with all the pent-up demand, prices are going to explode. So what's your estimate?"

Buyers: "We think it could drop fifty thousand dollars."

Agent: "Well let's see if we can buy it now for that 'next year price'. Plus are you just trying to time the pricing or are you also trying to time where you'd rather live?"

Buyers: "No, we still think we are going to wait till next year."

VERIFYING & REVERSING OBJECTIONS

This highly professional communication model not only gets to the truth immediately but it also can save an agent days or weeks of fruitlessly showing homes to Buyers who will not buy. This professional communication also provides an opportunity for the Buyer to more clearly see their options as it causes a more open and transparent expression of oftentimes concealed concerns and true timetables.

Here are a few more examples:

Buyers: "The kitchen is outdated" or "The ceilings are too low" or "We don't like the backyard there is no privacy" or "The taxes are too high"...

Agent: (Taxes objection) "If you were not concerned about the taxes ... let's say they were more to your liking ... then in your opinion do you feel this home might meet your needs?"

Buyers: "Possibly."

Agent: "The fact that the taxes are too low may be the reason to buy this amazing home. If the taxes were lower ... which are partially deductible ... the prices would probably be much higher and we would not have the world-class school system, the advantage to homeowners is that you don't need to pay for private school and the benefit is a world-class education in one of the counties most coveted communities (did you notice the FAB communication model?) Yet if you are interested, I will use the taxes when I negotiate for you."

SUMMARY

There are no magic words or strategies that can ever alter the destiny of a home purchase should the home not be right for the Buyers. The purpose of edu-selling is to learn what the true concerns are and provide potential solutions through more information, data, knowledge, wisdom, and therefore education. This edu-selling process increases the likelihood of a sale and also creates more open and trustworthy conversations.

NOTES

SEGMENT 5

HOW TO REACH FIRST-TIME BUYERS FIRST

There is arguably no segment of Home Buyers more in need of consultative, trusted advice (and more apt to recognize the invaluable assistance and overall value of a Buyer Agent) than first-time Buyers and yet, ironically, the time in which they need the most help is (in most cases) when they are not First-Time Buyers... but renters.

A classic definition of marketing is: 'Marketing means first determining the unmet needs of consumers and then creating goods and services to satisfy such needs'. Renters (before they can become Buyers) have needs that are underserved by the real estate industry in general. Validation of that assertion can be found in the following conventional real estate advertisement, "When you are ready to buy or sell a home give me a call!" The obvious implication here is the not-too-subtle message, "Until you are ready, do not call me!"

Renters have pronounced **unmet needs** that neither this conventional messaging reflects nor where the proper services that renters require are being presented. It is for this reason, that years ago, I created 'The Real Estate Renter to Buyer Assistance Program' for my brokerage. Before explaining how it worked, let me put into perspective its relevance and importance at that time to renters, sellers, developers, and our company agents.

The dean of the Harvard Business School once said:
Every businessperson must ask themselves two questions:

1) What do I do that my competitors do, that I do better?

2) What do I do that none of my competitors do?

Effectively responding to these simple yet critically important questions became an obsession of mine, as Joe Murphy and I grew a company to 32 owned and 60 regional marketing centers when our affiliate franchisees are included!

Competitors at that time were merely announcing, "We speak your language," as a way to address the diverse market we served, yet with no accompanying marketing or educational materials. Instead, we produced four-color Buyers Guides in six separate languages (alphabetically listed) in Chinese, English, Japanese, Korean, Russian, and Spanish. Agents in other companies referred to the 'importance of Feng Shui' while I created a **Feng Shui Division with its own director**! These are examples of either doing something better or doing something that no one else is doing.

The example of this consumer-centric strategy is reflected, for our purpose here in **Buyer Agent Be Aware**, to help Buyer Agents reach First-Time Buyers First... and last! Our 'Renter to Buyer Assistance Program' was something better than what our competitors were doing, because our competitors were simply imitating each other by just educating the already in-the-market 'First-Time Buyers'... and had no program to bring them into the market. This guidance was unnecessary as First-Time Buyers were already in the market to buy a home and had resolved that Buying was better than renting. Also, our competitors were doing First-Time Buyer Seminars without first reaching out to a **much larger and unbundled rental community.**

The **'Renter to Buyer Assistance Program'** enabled our company, and perhaps it might for you today (should you develop an updated and digital version of this concept), to accomplish the following:

1) By advertising (and through social media)... if you will forgive the colorful metaphor 'In Order to Tag the Fish Upstream'... and start Buyer Engagement higher up in the proverbial 'sales funnel' (or within 'your celebrated pipeline'.) **You will now be the first to get the First-Time Buyers.**

2) When asking Home Sellers, "Which segment of the market is the most likely demographic," and they respond, "First-Time Buyers," **you can explain your unique program.**

3) While competitors, as mentioned, occasionally conduct a First-Time Buyers Seminar (or Zoom meeting), you can create a 'Rent to Buy Assistance Program'. This branding will make it appear as though there must be **a new government program to help Renters become Buyers**, although we never presented this program in that fashion.

4) There are numerous rental buildings with residents who self-define being renters **and not First-Time Buyers**, therefore you can introduce a relevant service to an exponentially greater number of potential First-Time Buyer Clients.... entire rental buildings and communities.

5) You can secure more condo and townhouse developments by demonstrating to developers that **you can target entire rental communities** with a 'Rent to Buy Assistance Program' and encourage them to make painless concessions in order to produce a targeted campaign... such as 'The Ocean Estates Renter to Buyer Assistance Program', where the developer provides, again, necessary assistance or concessions.

How does the program work?

This concept and its recommended program, admittedly, works best in a so-called 'Buyers' Market'. At a time when builders or home sellers need to **do more to get homes sold** and not in markets (like now) where there is a shortage of inventory.

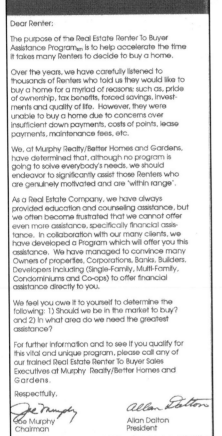

Dear Renter:

The purpose of the Real Estate Renter To Buyer Assistance Program℠ is to help accelerate the time it takes many Renters to decide to buy a home.

Over the years, we have carefully listened to thousands of Renters who told us they would like to buy a home for a myriad of reasons; such as, pride of ownership, tax benefits, forced savings, investments and quality of life. However, they were unable to buy a home due to concerns over insufficient down payments, costs of points, lease payments, maintenance fees, etc.

We, at Murphy Realty/Better Homes and Gardens, have determined that, although no program is going to solve everybody's needs, we should endeavor to significantly assist those Renters who are genuinely motivated and are 'within range'.

As a Real Estate Company, we have always provided education and counseling assistance, but we often become frustrated that we cannot offer even more assistance, specifically financial assistance. In collaboration with our many clients, we have developed a Program which will offer you this assistance. We have managed to convince many Owners of properties, Corporations, Banks, Builders, Developers including (Single-Family, Multi-Family, Condominiums and Co-ops) to offer financial assistance directly to you.

We feel you owe it to yourself to determine the following: 1) Should we be in the market to buy? and 2) In what area do we need the greatest assistance?

For further information and to see if you qualify for this vital and unique program, please call any of our trained Real Estate Renter To Buyer Sales Executives at Murphy Realty/Better Homes and Gardens.

Respectfully,

Joe Murphy
Chairman

Allan Dalton
President

That said, Renter-to-Buyer Assistance from Sellers who might wish to pay three months of a renter's remaining lease, pay a point, or provide a moving company (as every bit helps), should be considered.

ASK YOURSELF THESE QUESTIONS:

Are interest rates favorable?

How long should I wait to buy a home?

Are there many properties available in my price range?

What are the tax advantages of buying?

What type of property do I prefer? (single family, duplex, condo, co-op.)

Can I receive financial assistance?

A trained Murphy Realty/Better Homes and Gardens Sales Representative will help you with the answers to these questions and many other questions at no cost to you.

Assistance can also be in the form of educational assistance, expert Buyer Agent Counseling, and trusted advice (or even if a real estate brokerage decides to provide a little assistance in the form of lowering their negotiated fee)... and where this becomes the first step in creating loyal Clients-for-Life!

First-time Home Buyer education and Guidance Programs result in new homeowners only declaring, "We had a great Buyer Agent who helped us buy our first home!" These Clients instead will declare, "We decided to stop renting and buy, and are now homeowners, because of our great Buyer Agent and their Renter to Buyer Sales Program."

It's the difference between a First-Time Buyer finding a Buyer Agent vs a Buyer Agent finding a Renter and converting them into a First-Time Buyer.

The REAL ESTATE RENTER TO BUYER ASSISTANCE PROGRAM℠

I am interested in learning more about the Real Estate Renter to Buyer Assistance Program℠.

I may be reached at _____ during the day or _____ in the evenings. (Phone #)

Name: _____

Address: _____

City: _____ State: _____

Zip: _____

Murphy Sale Executive: _____

Call me at: _____

NOTES

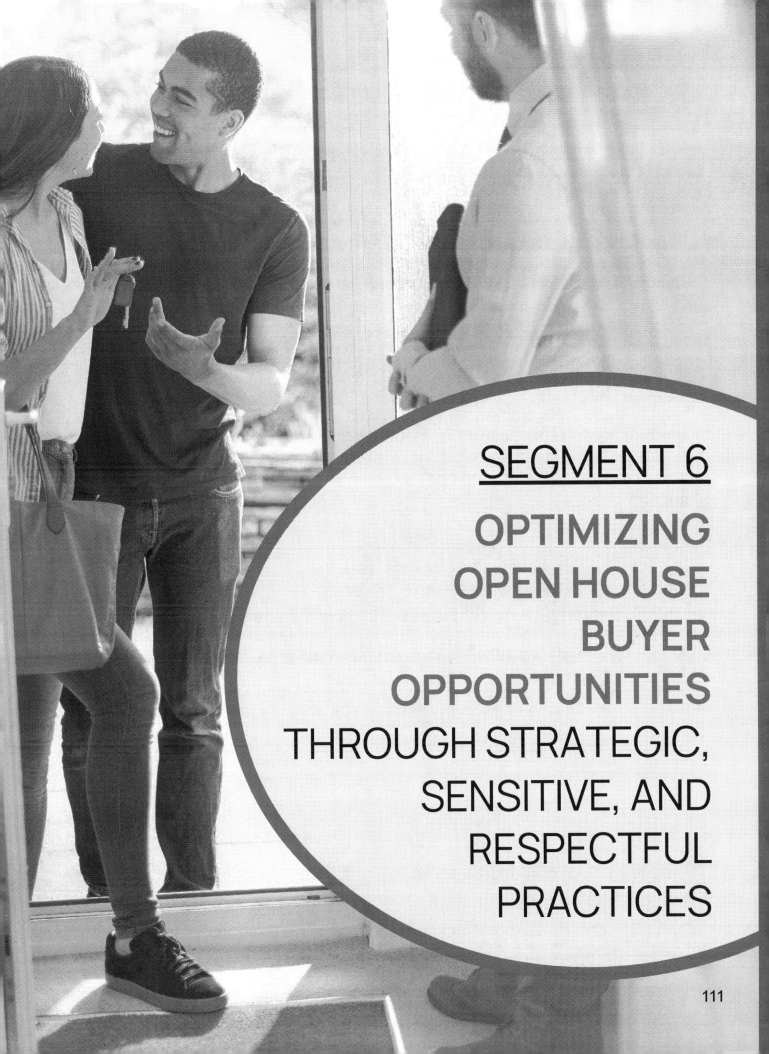

SEGMENT 6

OPTIMIZING OPEN HOUSE BUYER OPPORTUNITIES THROUGH STRATEGIC, SENSITIVE, AND RESPECTFUL PRACTICES

111

According to the National Association of Realtors®, **48%** of Buyers visit an open house.

Zillow research states that **72%** of home sellers in urban areas agree to an open house.

63% of sellers in suburban areas, and **47%** in rural regions also choose this conventional real estate marketing method.

Yet only **3 to 7 % of Buyers purchased the open house they visited**.

Such data suggests that open houses, although popular with sellers and Buyers, **may not be universally fruitful** for real estate professionals seeking to optimize the time and effort they expend at their open houses.

However, as discussed elsewhere in this program, because knowledge and wisdom are more valuable than information and data, successful real estate professionals have learned that well-conceived, constructed, marketed, and managed open houses can catapult them to remarkable and sustained success.

This is because open houses represent a **marketing magnet** designed to attract the following demographics (see below) as well as presenting a unique opportunity for real estate professionals to showcase their market knowledge, wisdom, communication skills, and ethics to future Buyers (and sellers).

Open House Visitors include but not limited to:
- Buyers
- Future Buyers
- Local Home Sellers
- Neighbors
- People Passing By
- Other Agents

Since every real estate agent hopefully and presumably has said that they are in a **people business**, then – just as the famous bank robber Willie Sutton once said that he robbed banks because "that is where the money is" – agents should also do open houses because that is **where the people are**. People that include **48% of actual Buyers** and Buyers who oftentimes have a **home to sell.**

Indeed, open houses represent the most **robust opportunity to meet complete strangers**, made less strange because the reason they are there is because of their **interest in real estate**...which also happens to be what you **sell and market for a living**. The more an agent believes in their preparation, communication, marketing, selling skill, and systematic follow-up the more they will enjoy **significant success** at an open house and the more excited and grateful they will become regarding open house opportunities.

Not to mention that it would be imprudent for real estate professionals to naively forego one of their few remaining high-touch opportunities.

When such confidence is developed and the potential of a **well-marketed, manicured and managed open house is imagined**, then the days will be passe where real estate professionals lamented "I have to **sit** an open house this weekend" (as if being punished) and instead will possess an attitude that positively focuses on **multi-dimensional real estate opportunities.**

Accordingly, your **open house mindset** – considering that only a small percentage of Buyers will purchase that specific home and that mathematically only one Buyer in fact ever will – means that equally important to Buyers being there to look and evaluate the home is that they will also be **looking at and evaluating you!** While the Buyers may not consciously realize that they are evaluating you – in the same way that they will be identifying "that this is the family room and this is the principal bedroom" – they subconsciously are (at the very least) noting the following features which speak to your appeal:

1) This is how the agent welcomed us
2) This is how they made us and our children feel comfortable
3) This is how they treated our pet
4) This is how they served their home seller client
5) This is how knowledgeable this agent is

While open house visitors are assessing the home, and where you may represent merely the secondary concern of Buyers, considering how few buy that home, **their assessment of you** may very well become **the most important evaluation they make during their visit!**

Like anything else, there is a right way and a wrong way to do all things.

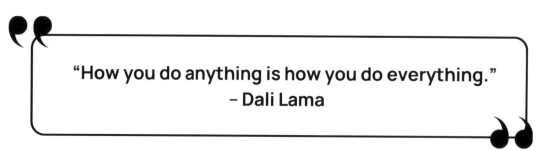

"How you do anything is how you do everything."
– Dali Lama

Marketing and managing open houses becomes a matter of the right strategy and attention to details.

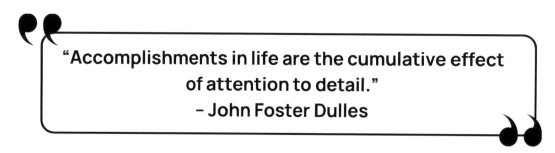

"Accomplishments in life are the cumulative effect of attention to detail."
– John Foster Dulles

Please consider what your present-day strategy is and its details regarding the following components required to optimize your open houses.

Please circle a response 1–5 with **5 being most effective**

How effective are you in explaining the benefits of an open house to home sellers?

1   2   3   4   5

How effective is your strategy to market your open house, including neighbors?

1   2   3   4   5

How effective is your market data? Company, brokerage, and team content?

1   2   3   4   5

How effectively do you communicate with Buyers at an open house?

1   2   3   4   5

How effectively do you follow up with Buyers from your open house?

1   2   3   4   5

How to explain to home sellers the reason for an open house:

- 48 percent of Buyers visit open houses.

- Higher-income Buyers are more likely to visit open houses.

- Many Buyers do not want to be accompanied by a salesperson.

- At open houses... this oftentimes gives me the greatest opportunity to communicate directly with the Buyer. If they do not come with an agent, because of how together we have created a 'lifestyle story' that I can now directly communicate the distinctiveness of your home to Buyers without interference from the Buyer agent. Remember, if the agent is representing the Buyer, they have an ethical responsibility only to their Buyer... which means, presumably, they will try to help their Buyer pay less... not to mention they will not have taken the time to make a Lifestyle Story narrative, which is vital.

- Having an open house enables me to also learn directly from Buyers what is important to them.

- Sometimes agents will not bring their Buyers to homes that they believe are not suitable. Yet many Buyers end up purchasing categories of homes they said they did not want to see. For example, they tell their Buyer Agents they only want to see Colonials but then on their own visit a Ranch home during an open house. Let us leave it up to the Buyers to decide and not just Buyer Agent decisions.

- Also, Buyers are traveling greater distances to look at homes post-COVID and this provides me the opportunity to also educate them in person regarding the community, schools, services, etc.

- I will be able to use ChalkDigital to geo-target where likely Buyers are coming from.

Strategies to market an open house including neighbors:
(recommendations and checklist)

- Door hangers to neighbors' homes

- Knock on neighbors' doors to invite and explain why there might be additional traffic on the street.

- Invite neighbors to visit one-half hour early for a special open house for neighbors (by either knocking on doors or calling).

- Open house signs to the geographical and numerical limits allowed.

- Open house sign at end of the street.

- Signs should go up on Thursday for weekend open houses.

- Open house hours should be different times on different days.

- Open house announcement on social media:
  - Reels
  - Tik Tok
  - Instagram
  - LinkedIn, etc.

- Open house bulletin through your CRM

- Open house prospects tagged by special requirements i.e. near the beach, near the schools, etc. (make sure all tags are legal)

- BombBomb™ video email announcements

- Use ChalkDigital to geo-target Buyers

- Create a custom OPEN HOUSE Welcome Mat

Content-rich Open Houses

Remember there is a reason why doctor and dentist offices display "take one" brochures. Consumers and clients are interested in the overall value these professionals represent. Real estate is no different. It is advisable that you **provide the following content to open houses**:

A long-form **Community Video** doesn't work on Social Media but is extremely impactful with Buyers seriously considering the Town and craving more relevant, convenient information
(note: this is an active QR code. Watch the Video)

Create a business-size card with **five facts about the home on the front**: square footage, picture of home, price, size of lot, and address.
On the back, QR codes - one for Lifestyle Stories, one for your website (note: not active links)

Create **Lifestyle Stories** to better educate Buyers (note: QR code is active)

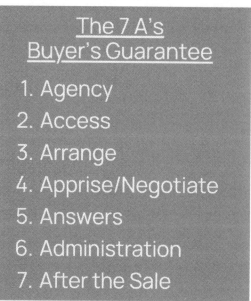

The 7 A's
Buyer's Guarantee

1. Agency
2. Access
3. Arrange
4. Apprise/Negotiate
5. Answers
6. Administration
7. After the Sale

Communicating with Open House Visitors

1) **Don't let visitors ring the bell or knock on the door.** Instead beat guests to the punch – open the door and personally and warmly greet them.

Purpose:
This breaks down the barrier and awkwardness of the door and creates a sense that you enthusiastically welcome them. Plus it establishes control (in the professional and personal and not pejorative sense of the word).

2) **Don't ask visitors to sign in** unless they instinctively move over to the sign-in table. Start thinking of the sign-in sheet as both a sign-in OR **sign-out sheet**.

Purpose:
Because many people find this immediate requirement or request intrusive or uncomfortable, they often times record their names either illegible or incorrectly. This means they have memorialized that they can never have ongoing contact, either due to their false information or unwillingness to become exposed for their deception... they feel forced to remain evasive or uncooperative.

3) "Before you begin your tour of the home, folks, there are a few important features and facts about the home that are not obvious, and if you like, later I can review them when you like."

Purpose:
When this is said at the very beginning, it relieves all of the feelings that they must first "go through TSA-like security". Once this anxiety is avoided and they know they are free to go independently on their tour of the home, it changes all of the interpersonal dynamics. Consequently, the likelihood of gaining trust and accurate contact information exponentially increases.

Communicating with Open House Visitors (Cont.)

4) "Are you familiar with this area?"

Purpose:

Rather than asking "Are you new to the area?" which can come across as similar to meeting with an immigration official, this question is considerably more appropriate and comfortable for open house visitors (allows try to place yourself in their shoes).

5) Never ask at the very beginning "Are you working with another agent?"

Purpose:

This sounds as if their answer might exclude them from seeing the home or that your helpfulness is conditional. A little later, during the visit and within the questionnaire or earlier on during agency disclosure, this must be covered.

6) "You might be interested in...". As you begin to get to know the Buyers and establish greater trust and comfort, you can learn if they are relocating, moving up, downsizing, have children, pets, etc., and then introduce relevant content brochures.

Purpose:

You only want to introduce content after you have uncovered an interest.

7) What is your timetable for moving to a new home?

Purpose:

After rapport has been established, rather than saying "When do you want to, or have to buy?", which sounds too sales-focused, merely asking about their timetable is more expansive yet accomplishes the same thing.

Communicating with Open House Visitors (Cont.)

8) Don't ask, "What do you like about the home?"

Purpose:
That suggests there might be things they do not like.

9) "My home sellers always ask me whenever possible to get feedback. Would you mind sharing your first and overall general impressions?"

Purpose:
This is also the gateway to learning more about the needs of the Buyers.

10) Never say anything to the Buyers (or anyone else) that diminishes, compromises, or is disrespectful to your home seller clients.

Purpose:
The way you ethically and professionally represent your seller clients will be inferred by future Buyer or seller clients as how you will represent them if they don't buy that home - or either buy or sell a home with you. An example of what to never say to a consumer, other client, or other agent: "My sellers are going through a divorce." Unless and only if it is this way, "My sellers are going through a divorce, and they have authorized me to reveal this."

11) Only after significant comfort and mutual respect (and likability has been attained)... "May I ask... do you have either children or pets like the home sellers do?"

Purpose:
So you can present - at the conclusion of the tour - your guides or you can ask them if you can email them - which is another way of getting their email address.

Communicating with Open House Visitors (Cont.)

12) Incidentally folks, during your home search if you drive by or see online any neighborhood or home that you find very desirable, even if it's not on the market, I would be very happy to contact the homeowners and see if they have any plans in the near future to sell... or if, with the right opportunity, would they sell right now.

Purpose:

Deepen your value to the Buyers and create additional listing opportunities

13) Since you are new to the area, I'd like you to know that one of the services I provide to many homeowners within the community is my preferred vendors 'Maintenence and Property Management Directory".

Purpose:

Another way to validate you want to be their agent for life by providing an example of your invaluable service.

WELCOME TO OUR OPEN HOUSE!

Date_____   Open House Address: _____

NAME(S): _____

EMAIL: _____

PHONE: _____

ADDRESS: _____

_____

May I contact or email you any listings that may appeal to you *before* they come on the market?   Yes   No

Are You Working with an Agent?   Yes   No

Name of Your Agent: _____

COMFORTABLE PRICE RANGE:

☐ Under $500,000   ☐ $1,000,000 - $1,300,000

☐ $500,000 - $800,000   ☐ $1,300,000 - $1,500,000

☐ $800,000 - $1,000,000   ☐ $1,500,000—$2,000,000

NEEDS/ MUST HAVES:

Square Feet _____   Other _____

Bedrooms _____   Other _____

Baths _____   Other _____

HOW DID YOU HEAR OF OUR OPEN HOUSE TODAY?

☐ FACEBOOK   ☐ INSTAGRAM

☐ YOUTUBE   ☐ EMAIL NEWSLETTER

☐ ZILLOW   ☐ REALTOR.COM

☐ TRULIA   ☐ OTHER:_____

☐ DRIVE-BY   ☐ OTHER:_____

Open House Follow-Up Checklist

_____ Put Follow-Up in CRM

_____ Send Thank You Email

_____ Mailed Thank You Card with Business Card of the home
(inserted in the card) and a picture of the home.
When you write the thank you note include personal comments from your
interaction or the information from the Buyer's survey.

_____ Called Them

_____ Send a community video (if you have done one).

_____ Send VR Tour (if you have done one).

_____ Looked them up on Google / Facebook / LinkedIn

_____ Set them up for Market Updates

_____ Send BombBomb™ (or other video) thanking them
with a link/QR code to your brochure or Lifestyle Story Flip Book.

_____ Set them up for Auto Emails

_____ Put in Task for Follow-up Schedule

_____ Send referral to Mortgage Lender

_____ Researched Non-MLS and Expired Listings; FSBO's

_____ If represented by another agent, make a "just wanted to let you
know" phone call to their agent and provide feedback.

_____ Send a Lifestyle Story Flip Book link to their agent.

_____ Send a link to your Buyer's Guarantee
(included in this program)

Discussion Points (for Real Estate Teams and Offices):

- How important do you think open houses are?

- How would you want to be treated If you were a customer?

- Do you contact neighbors and invite them for a special showing?

- Do you think open house door hangers are a good idea?

- Do you like the idea of having a business-size card about the house?

- Do you like the idea of giving Buyers the choice of signing in or signing out or doing neither?

- How and when do introduce Buyer representation?

- How and when do you ask if they are working with someone else?

- Do you have a Buyers survey?

- Do you bring your content/guides?

- Do you always call all agents and if so, how soon after the open house?

- Do you send a video (and VR Tour) to all visitors?

- Do you send out an invitation en masse through your CRM?

- Do you create a custom OPEN HOUSE Welcome Mat?

- Do you have your Community Video paying on a loop on the open house TV?

Discussion Points (for Real Estate Teams and Offices):

- Do you wait until they ring the doorbell, or if possible open the door and greet them?

- How valuable do you think open houses are?

- Do you go door to door asking for neighborhood testimonials and present at your open houses (and to prospect future listings)?

- What will you do differently if anything, after reviewing this information?

_____

_____

_____

_____

Post Open House Debriefing:

Did I provide door hangers to neighbors?

| YES | NO |

Did I send special neighbor invitation?

| YES | NO |

Did I use CRM for target distribution?

| YES | NO |

Did I use social media?

| YES | NO |

Did I bring updated market data?

| YES | NO |

Did I bring content?

| YES | NO |

Did I step outside to greet visitors?

| YES | NO |

Did I send a follow up video?

| YES | NO |

Did I contact the visitor's agent where applicable?

| YES | NO |

Did I tell Buyers to let me know if there are any homes not on the market that they might be interested in?

| YES | NO |

Did I send thank-you notes?

| YES | NO |

Did I include QR code?

| YES | NO |

Did I provide home seller with a full overview of the results?

| YES | NO |

During the section in this program devoted to **Working With and For Luxury Buyers**, included will be concepts regarding that niche market and also how it relates to **Open House marketing**... including possible civic and charitable-related Open House events and the importance of world-class materials and photography.

SPECIAL THANKS to Julie Vanderblue and The Vanderblue Team for their significant contribution to the content found in the open house segment!

NOTES

_____

_____

_____

_____

_____

_____

_____

_____

_____

SEGMENT 7

THE TRUTH ABOUT BUYER LEAD GENERATION

You may recall an infamous scene from the film **Glengarry Glen Ross** where, in a sales presentation, Alec Baldwin tortures the company's sales teams with disparaging remarks regarding their pitiful sales results. If you watched the movie, you'll recall how the beleaguered and belittled sales team defended their failures. They all focused on one word:

LEADS

Leads indeed was the operative word – not that there weren't enough leads but rather they focused on the fact they had "low-quality leads".

This segment will examine, in part, the world of Buyer-side lead generation... as clearly, leads and lead gen, enjoy great relevance in the world of real estate sales as well.

I say "in part" because it is not my intent in this mere segment to attempt to deal comprehensively with this subject yet, at the same time, this report would be lacking in its coverage of Buyer-side elements if it were to completely ignore Buyer-side lead gen.

First, a personal observation:

When I became CEO of Realtor.com (a real estate website that is an important player within the lead gen universe), I immediately "sunset" a program that my predecessors had defined as "I-lead". The reason I terminated I-lead was because our research revealed that the number one reason agents were canceling their subscriptions to Realtor.com was because of the unacceptable 'caliber of leads' they were receiving.

This reaction was understandable, as back then, the industry not only had a massive misunderstanding of the difference between 'internet leads' and their prior world of 'off-line referrals' ... but also the technology wasn't as advanced nor as accepted as it is today in order to properly manage and covert 'leads'.

Prior to Realtor.com, 'off-line leads' were called 'referrals' from friends, families, and other agents or leads from the newspaper, open houses, or walk-ins (where the Buyer had taken overt actions to engage). Another contributor to the lack of lead appreciation years ago was the absence of text, emails, and less optimized and less functional CRMs. When one considers macro statistics, it also reveals why 'inquiries and leads' versus 'referrals' (while wanted) also caused disappointment.

Case in point: the last stats I saw from Google cite that they received 13 billion real estate searches that year. Of note is that there are typically no more than approximately five million transactions a year. The astonishing difference between inquiries/leads and sales set the foundation for massive frustration.

Yet now due to algorithms, A.I., real estate teams, call centers, CRMs, emails and texts, lead management processes can mitigate much of the endless frustrations surrounding lead management... and because lead expectations have become more realistically established in advance of agreeing to lead gen business models.

Pre-decision educational concepts such as cost-per-impression, per-click, per-conversion, per-contract, and the lifetime value of a Client acquired have reset the entire manner in which agents approach this subject... **one now with a focus and appreciation of metrics.**

It is unfortunate for the real estate industry that it lacked the capabilities to preempt Buyers (and now sellers) from being engaged first by non-real estate professionals, even though these same consumers would have ended up with real estate agents should these business models not exist. Moreover, even with all of the ever-increasing lead gen technology, the number of transactions (notwithstanding the surge in population) has not increased. What has changed is the exponential cost absorbed by hard-working and straight commission-compensated real estate professionals to just do business.

I was fearful of these consequences years ago and, in fact, I forewarned the industry (if that sounds pompous forgive me) in an outspoken fashion... as I will now recall.

Approximately twenty years ago, the founder of WebMD (the then CEO of Homestore, now Move Inc.) and I were interviewed in a production named **"Say No To Real Estate Tariffs!"**

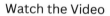
Watch the Video

The premise of the video was that Lawyers and Doctors were not paying referral fees to people or "paying for non-professional third-party referrals." Yet these third-party companies were imposing a "tariff" for Realtors® to acquire "real estate leads" (or referrals) even though those Third Parties weren't in any way increasing the number of Buyers or Sellers!

In 2024 and beyond, the "tariff genie" is out of the proverbial bottle! So, let's first examine some of the ways that agents can generate leads and individually benefit.

Yes, the industry at large (in my view) doesn't benefit when "outside sources" engage Buyers before Realtors® do.

Exercise

Please identify **how much value** (in terms of generating Buyer leads) you find in each of the following lead-generating sources:

	None	Somewhat	Meaningful
Open Houses	☐	☐	☐
Buyer Seminars	☐	☐	☐
Door Knocking	☐	☐	☐
Telemarketing	☐	☐	☐
Zoom Presentations	☐	☐	☐
Direct Mail	☐	☐	☐
BombBomb Video	☐	☐	☐
CRM	☐	☐	☐
Referrals from Clients	☐	☐	☐
Referrals from Friends	☐	☐	☐
Referrals from Other agents	☐	☐	☐
Cable Ads	☐	☐	☐
Radio	☐	☐	☐
Billboards	☐	☐	☐
Park Benches	☐	☐	☐
Supermarket Carriages	☐	☐	☐
Civic Organizations	☐	☐	☐
House of Worship	☐	☐	☐
SEO	☐	☐	☐
SOI	☐	☐	☐

Zillow Premiere ☐ ☐ ☐

Zillow Flex ☐ ☐ ☐

Google pay-per-click ☐ ☐ ☐

Homes.com ☐ ☐ ☐

Community Testimonial Prospecting ☐ ☐ ☐

Real Geeks ☐ ☐ ☐

Market Leader ☐ ☐ ☐

Other Lead Gen Companies

_____ ☐ ☐ ☐

_____ ☐ ☐ ☐

_____ ☐ ☐ ☐

_____ ☐ ☐ ☐

Other Sources

_____ ☐ ☐ ☐

_____ ☐ ☐ ☐

_____ ☐ ☐ ☐

_____ ☐ ☐ ☐

Which technology-based lead gen programs are the best?

There is no clear winner when it comes to which model is the best, because there are too many variables, and none of the variables equally apply to individual agents, in different markets, with different budgets, and different alternatives.gents, in different markets, with different budgets, and different alternatives. Yet, here are some considerations as you continue to re-evaluate and refine your "lead generation business plan".

1) Since lead gen-provided leads overwhelmingly come from online search engines and through social media platforms, let's review how much traffic each major site listed below commands.

Google attracts 13 Billion real estate searches
(which is almost double the world's population)

Zillow – 353 million users

Realtor.com – 133 million users

Homes.com – 39 million

Questions for Discussion

If you (as a knowledgeable real estate agent, **yet now a Buyer**) were searching for a new home, mortgage, or home remodeling where would you start?

Questions for Discussion (Cont.)

If you were to search for a real estate property or real estate-related content, would you be more likely to search on **the most visited websites listed previously** or would you revert to one of the social media sites you participate in, such as some of the following (if so, state why):

Facebook _____

LinkedIn _____

Tik Tok _____

Instagram _____

YouTube _____

Now that question does not make a distinction between those people who are "Searching" for content versus consumers (and especially Buyers) in which content or real estate agents are searching for them on social media sites.

People who you know, and who already know you, are more likely to be reached by you through social media platforms. Buyers who do not know you, including those you reach through buying ads on Facebook, represent a different level of interest when they are "being sought after" versus "those who search" on search engines and real estate websites of their own volition.

In advertising, they speak in terms of aided and unaided responses. Buyers can also be divided into those **already interested** or those who are "persuadable".

Just because a site attracts billions or hundreds of millions of real estate-interested and specific search visitors does not necessarily **translate to a benefit to agents who pay for leads.**

Why?

Just as real estate salespeople talk about a "sales funnel" theirs is a continuum or degree of increasingly intense Buyer search online. This means that not all levels of Buyer search interest have the same value.

Now because of algorithms and AI. Search engines and major portals like Zillow can also identify the relative interest of Buyers. Identifying Buyer's interest and readiness online (based upon clicking behavior) enables these sites' lead gen models to be able to retarget and re-market to these Buyers. For example, someone not only clicking on "homes for sale" but also "closing costs" and "moving companies" is treated differently than someone who merely clicks on "homes for sale".

Regathering and remarketing to these Buyers can also be accomplished through CRMs and lead gem company management. There are several outstanding lead gen choices so let's consider just a few of the top ones:

Zillow Premier

This program is open to all real estate agents yet there is a limit to the number of agents allowed per zip code. Also, premiere agents are expected to exercise rapid follow-up to leads. It is a monthly fee with a contract.

Zillow Flex

(I believe must be arraigned through a brokerage)

Zillow intelligently recognized that the credibility and integrity of their lead conversion (the industry average is about 5%) would enjoy a better outcome if the leads were distributed or directed (through their profiles) to real estate agents who were optimizing their CRMs. Therefore, these agents would ensure exemplary follow-up. Moreover, Flex agents represent the most successful agents at closing sales and have the most impressive bios and profiles. Clearly, these are the agents that Zillow desires to handle as many of the leads as possible.

Zillow Flex is a program where the top paying agent is willing to pay a fee yet on the condition that they only pay that fee when the Buyer's home closes. The benefit of this program is that there is no payment unless there is success, this is why it is called a "success fee". One has to be selected for this program and many top producers have reached out to their Zillow sales rep for information. Flex Agents, as well as Premiere Agents, can partake in the Zillow lead gen and management training. Another benefit (one underutilized) is that both Premiere Agents and Flex Agents can not only leverage their decision to acquire, engage, serve, and sell Buyers when presenting to or proposing to home sellers … but can also announce their "special status" on social media or through a press release.

For example, how many agents do the following that I recommend:

Consumer or friend: Hey, Susan! How is everything going with your real estate business?

Susan: I don't know if you know this but I was recently selected as a Zillow Flex Agent.

Consumer: What the heck is that?

Susan: You have heard of Zillow, I'm sure. Well, they select only the most accomplished agents to receive their Buyer leads in many of the most important markets.

Consumer: Wow!

Susan: I know it might not mean much unless you are looking to sell your home someday but I thought you'd like to know. Anytime you see Zillow advertised tell me who you'll think about.

Calling Expireds

Susan: Was there some reason you wanted to market your home without a Zillow Premier Agent? Just so you know, I am the Zillow Flex Agent that covers this zip code and I will be using lead gen systems to advertise for new construction Buyers.

Ed. note

This is also why you want to move lead gen traffic to your website and CRM by telling them, otherwise their data is going to be sold to a number of agents when they go to these portals instead of seeing all properties on IDX on your website.

Realtor.com "Connections"

Agents can buy a portion of leads within zip codes. There are usually other agents who have also bought a piece of that zip code. Because multiple agents are involved this means that your profile, bio, and speed to respond are vital. Essentially this business model recreates an "Olympic-like race to the gold", causing response and profile wars.

Realtor.com also has "Connections Plus"

agents pay more and claim all of the leads within a geographical area.

Looking at the Top 2 websites and their lead gen offers... a few thoughts jump out:

1. The rich get richer – in Zillow Flex, the agents who have less money and fewer clients or prospects (who would be the most willing to accept a success fee-only model for the most part) do not have that opportunity.

2 . The lower producing agents who have Zillow Premiere are also less likely to be fully optimizing the immediate follow-up, retargeting, and remarketing opportunities to compete in follow-up needs or satisfy the ongoing performance standards of either Zillow Premiere or Realtor.com's Connections Plus.

3 . Less successful agents are less likely to have developed a lead management infrastructure, have team leaders with administrative support, or run teams with dedicated Buyer Agents. Therefore they think less in terms of the lifetime value of a client.

A classic example of how leads are as valuable as you can make them is captured in the following example:

When I first arrived at Realtor.com brokerages could not be clients or advertise all of their listings. When I created a program called "company showcase" the brokerages who were the happiest were those that had lead routing, lead management systems, and mortgage and insurance companies To these companies, the value of a lead (and over the lifetime of that Buyer) was invaluable.

Google claims the following (from my Google search lol):

1) Google pay-per-click leads to the following results:

- Their click rate – 6.11 %
- The real estate industry – 9.09 %

2) Cost per click:

- Google – $1.55
- Real Estate – $4.22

3) 74 % of people who click will also answer their phone

Google helps target Buyers through the following targeting:

- Demographic targeting: age, income, etc.

- Affinity targeting: "What Buyers have been searching for"

- Customized Keywords

- Life Changing Events

- Re-marketing: reaching out again to Buyers who previously clicked ads

- Location: geographical placement

The four types of Google real estate ads:

1) Search

2) Display

3) Video

4) Local Service

Google claims the following (from my Google search lol):

1) Google pay-per-click leads to the following results:

- Their click rate – 6.11 %
- The real estate industry – 9.09 %

2) Cost per click:

- Google – $ 1.55
- Real Estate – $ 4.22

3) 74 % of people who click will also answer their phone

Google helps target Buyers through the following targeting:

- Demographic targeting: age, income, etc.

- Affinity targeting: "What Buyers have been searching for"

- Customized Keywords

- Life Changing Events

- Re-marketing: reaching out again to Buyers who previously clicked ads

- Location: geographical placement

The four types of Google real estate ads:

1) Search

2) Display

3) Video

4) Local Service

What is interesting about these **Top 10 search terms** is how the top priorities consumers indicate have to do with **taking action**... and that requires **knowledge more than data or information**:

- "Homes" to buy Homes

- "Mortgage" to secure a mortgage

- "Rent versus buy" – Educate and sell me!

- "Affordable Housing" – I need help!

- "First-time Buyers" – I need help more than info.

- "Real Estate agents" – Who can help me?

- "Home Equity" – I need money.

- "Foreclosure" – I need help!

- "Market Date" – Should we buy, sell, or stay?

- "Closing Costs" – Getting ready to buy.

Summary

Since someone has already written a full book or does a weeks-long training class on Facebook, LinkedIn, YouTube, Instagram, other social media platforms, and lead gen, I am not including social media lead gen.

I also have not included detailed information on Homes.com and their epic lead gent concept of "Your listing Your lead". I encourage you to investigate lead gen giants like **Real Geeks**, **Market Leader**, and many others.

What I want to emphasize most is that I believe the number one lead gen system is your CRM. This is because a high percentage of Buyers already live within 20 miles of where you live and work which means the homesellers you would ever represent live within 20 miles of where you work... and these listings end up generating Buyers.

Increasingly, Buyers will go **directly to the listing agent** or visit without representation at your open house. Listings will always generate Buyers more than Buyers will generate listings. **The Majority of sellers end up buying in the same market.**

A few years ago, one of my former agents made over a million dollars mostly from postcards. She measured the cost of her postcard campaigns versus all major lead generation models and concluded that her ROI was far better through her postcard campaigns.

Lead gen also means appreciating that "SOI" (sphere of influence) alone does not generate leads...but influences your sphere. **Most top producers appreciate that lead gen is multi-dimensional.**

Discussion / Questions

What percentage of the leads (that end up on your CRM) come from these different sources and how much do you invest in each?

Google   _____

Zillow   _____

Realtor.com   _____

Other Websites   _____

Lead Gen Companies   _____

Door-knocking   _____

Direct Mail   _____

Postcards   _____

Telemarketing   _____

Clients   _____

Open Houses   _____

Other Agent Referrals   _____

YouTube   _____

Facebook   _____

Instagram   _____

LinkedIn   _____

Tik Tok   _____

Other Social Media   _____

TV   _____

Radio   _____

Newspapers   _____

Seminars   _____

Zoom Meetings   _____

Networking Through Organizations   _____

Houses of Worship   _____

Civic Organizations   _____

I respectfully suggest you consider each lead gen source listed (and others not listed) to create your **Lead Gen Business Plan**.

NOTES

SELLING
NEW CONSTRUCTION
& EFFECTIVE
USE OF VIDEO

An interview with
accomplished team leader,
Andrew Undem

A word about Andrew Undem:

In a later segment of **Buyer Agent Be Aware,** I share marketing strategies I developed and used to help secure major developments while also being responsible for my company's attracting and servicing new construction Buyers. Since the examples I used (although still forward-looking) are from the past... I thought, "Who better than to engage regarding modern-day new construction purchasing than Andrew Undem? Andrew, at the age of 34 had already developed and led one of the top five real estate teams in his brand's global network. Andrew co-authored with me **34 Proclamations** and is in high demand to speak at important industry events. I asked Andrew to contribute information for **BUYER AGENT BE AWARE** that both Buyer Agents and Buyers of New Construction will find invaluable.

●···●

New Home Construction is a significant market for both home Buyers and Buyers Agents. At the time of this writing (2024), 33% of all listings are new homes. New home PURCHASING represents a different process. This is because Buyers are not negotiating with a traditional Seller but rather a **home builder** who has many other homes to sell and who possesses a higher level of vigilance regarding profit.

There are many benefits to new homes. Typically there are few multiple offer scenarios (at least in my greater Baltimore market) and, therefore, full price is almost always accepted. Everything is under warranty. The homes are built to the latest building codes which makes them extremely energy efficient and cuts down on maintenance costs.

It is imperative to remember that, when dealing with the new home representative who is representing the builder, you want to make them your ally. They do not own the homes, they simply want to sell them. By establishing greater rapport with the new homes' sales rep, you can gather key information that will help you fully understand the value of the homes and how to leverage the information they provide as you consider purchasing a new home. Remember: great Buyer Agents and Buyers get rewarded for the information they gather, not the information they give.

This segment will help your Buyer with some of the basics to ensure that both you and them are well-informed and armed with **the proper questions to ask as you consider new home communities.**

Some key areas to fully understand in any new home community are the area map, site plan (homesites), floor plan options, current builder incentives, the builder/developer relationship, and the current sales pace and pricing history.

Area Map

In each new home community, you will normally see an "area map" that showcases where the homes will be built in relation to the surrounding areas. It's always wise to study what else is going on in the area in terms of other new developments and existing housing stock, along with ease of access to commercial amenities and commuter routes.

Questions to ask:

Where are most of the Buyers coming from who buy here? Are there any major employers close by? Where is the closest grocery store? What new amenities are coming to the area? Which school zone will this community feed? What's the typical price appreciation in this zip code over the last 10 years?

Site Plan

The site plan is a drawing showing the exact number of homes to be built, where they are built, and the size of the lots. There are several nuances to the site plan that include what type of house can be built on what homesite, the exact size and slope of each lot, and what the homes face and back up to. Often there are premium homesites that are bigger, flatter, and back to woods that the builder will want a premium for. This, like all financial aspects of putting a deal together, is always negotiable.

Questions to ask:

How many total homes will be in the community? Is there a mix of condos, townhomes, and single-family homes? Are there any premium homesites? Which phases will be built first? Are there certain homesites that only accommodate certain floor plans? When do you anticipate selling out the community? How long will there be construction taking place in the area?

Floor Plans

New home communities typically offer 4-6 different floor plans in a community. The model home is normally the floor plan that sells the most. Knowing what your needs are will help you dial in which floor plan is best for you. The floor plans are self-explanatory but sometimes the pricing between floor plans is not. The devil is in the details!

Questions to ask:

What is the difference in price / square foot between each floor plan? What options are included in the list price? What options are available? Do you have a full sheet of pricing options for the non-standard options? What are the most common upgrades selected? Where can I see a finished version of the XYZ floor plan?

Current Builder Incentives

Builders almost always offer incentives to "buy now". They typically offer $ towards closing costs or "free options". It is very important to understand what the builder's current incentives are and how they've changed over the last few months. If a community is selling homes quickly, the pricing will go up and incentives go down. If they arent selling at the pace they planned for, pricing may go down but normally they keep prices steady and instead, increase the incentives so they do not hurt the "comps" in the neighborhood. It is common practice for builders to tie in their own mortgage and title company to the incentive package as a way for them to recoup some revenue for the incentive to entice Buyers to "act now". A savvy Buyer & Buyer Agent can typically negotiate bigger incentives if they know the right questions to ask.

Questions to ask:

Are the current incentives tied to a specific mortgage and or title company? Can I still get the incentive if I use my own mortgage company? How have the incentives changed over the last 6 months? How many homes are selling a month on average? What is the largest incentive the builder has offered in this community? If my mortgage company offers a better rate, can I use them and still get the incentive package?

Builder / Developer Relationship

Just because the builder is building and selling homes in a community does not necessarily mean they own the land. Sometimes builders buy lots from a developer who owns the land, other times the builder buys the raw land and turns it into buildable lots which makes the builder and developer one and the same. In the case where the builder is not the developer, you can uncover some information that may aid your side of the negotiations.

Questions to ask:

Did your company develop this land or are you buying finished lots from the developer? Are there any other builders coming into the community or do you have exclusivity? Is there a "lot takedown schedule in place"? (A lot take-down schedule dictates how many lots the builder must buy per month or quarter from the developer. If you can determine how many lots they must buy / month and factor that in with their current sales space you will be able to tell if they are ahead or behind schedule. If they are behind they will be more flexible when negotiating pricing and incentives). What will the community look like when it's finished? Are there any sidewalks, green space, walking trails or additional trees to be planted once the community is nearing completion?

New Home Builders provide a wonderful option for many home Buyers. The Buyers and Buyer Agents who understand the process, and cast of characters involved in the new home construction side, will always be able to get a better deal. Remember - the new home sales rep is your friend. They will answer your questions and if they don't know the answer they can get them from their sales manager. If the sales manager doesn't know it will escalate to a VP or Division president who is normally the decision maker on whether they will accept or reject an offer. If you can get to the truth quickly and maintain rapport with the builder representative - **you will come out on top.**

For more detailed information or for Buyer or Seller referrals in Greater Baltimore, please do not hesitate to contact me! Andrew Undem – andrew@SUREsalesgroup.com

CRAIG PROCTOR'S PERSPECTIVE

The Future of Buyer Commissions

AN UPDATE

The NAR's agreement to settle the multitude of class action lawsuits by paying $418 million in damages and eliminating its rules on commissions has real estate agents asking themselves a good question: "How will I get paid"? You must be informed about what's at stake, how it will impact you and what you can and should do to insulate your business against these changes.

(Scan Code for the Report)

CRAIG PROCTOR CONTINUED

The reason why I decided to provide a link to Craig Proctor's very comprehensive report, **The Future of Buyer Commissions**, is to fill an obvious void within **BUYER AGENT BE AWARE**. Specifically, while I state on the front of this book/resource, "What Every Buyer Agent Must Do In a Post-Disrupted Real Estate World," I purposefully avoid (as do my contributors) any reference to what has caused this universally recognized disruption, and any thoughts or suggestions regarding commissions, other than to repeat what I always said, "That all commissions are always negotiable." Yet, while I have avoided these subjects, the readers of my book cannot avoid the direct impact these 'controversial' issues will have on their respective careers regarding how they individually present value and 'negotiate' Buyer/Client fees.

Accordingly, I thank Craig Proctor for both tackling these issues (which solely represent his opinions and perspectives) and for granting me the permission to inform my readers (even though this report is being widely distributed in the public domain), that this extremely relevant content and advice is easily accessible to them as a free download (see QR code below).

I also would be remiss not to acknowledge what distinguishes Craig Proctor as a world-class coach... one who belongs on the Mount Rushmore of real estate coaches: Craig has packaged a level of strategic-based and practical 'systems' that are transferrable to anyone and everyone. The business practices that he engineered and implemented, which led him to become the number one agent in the entire ReMaxx Global Network not once but twice, he makes available to his forward-thinking and deeply appreciative network of successful real estate agents. Regardless of what you think of his report (some of which I disagree with), you will immediately recognize a level of insight, nuanced thinking, innovation, clarity, and courageous insights that make Craig a true industry treasure.

– Thank you, Craig.

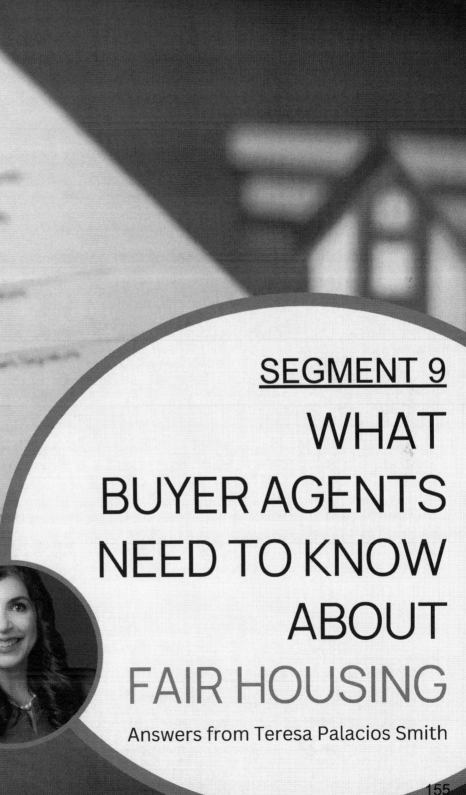

SEGMENT 9

WHAT BUYER AGENTS NEED TO KNOW ABOUT FAIR HOUSING

Answers from Teresa Palacios Smith

A word about Teresa Palacios Smith:

Teresa Palacios Smith represents the Gold Standard regarding advancing adherence to Fair Housing Laws. Teresa is the president of NAHREP (National Association of Hispanic Real Estate Professionals), Chief Diversity, Equity & Inclusion Officer for HomeServices of America and HSF Affiliates, and the creator and host of the WOMEN WHO LEAD podcast. Teresa has educated tens of thousands of real estate professionals and scores of brokerages on why diversity, equity, and inclusion is not only a legal and ethical must but also a money maker.

•••

What should real estate professionals know about Fair Housing laws as it relates to Buyers?

Real estate professionals should understand Fair Housing laws to ensure they are not involved in any discriminatory practices when working with Buyers. This includes understanding protected classes, such as race, color, religion, sex, national origin, familial status, and disability. They should know that it is against the law to discriminate against Buyers based on any of these protected characteristics when selling or renting properties. In addition, members of the National Association of REALTORS® (NAR®) adhere to a code of ethics which also states that discrimination based on gender and sex is also prohibited.

The NAR's Code of Ethics is a set of professional standards that real estate agents and brokers voluntarily agree to abide by as members of the association.

The specific provision in the NAR Code of Ethics that addresses discrimination is Standard of Practice 10-3, which states: "REALTORS® shall not deny equal professional services to any person for reasons of race, color, religion, sex, handicap, familial status, national origin, sexual orientation, or gender identity. REALTORS® shall not be parties to any plan or agreement to discriminate against a person or persons on the basis of race, color, religion, sex, handicap, familial status, national origin, sexual orientation, or gender identity."

This provision aligns with the principles of fair housing and non-discrimination, and it reinforces the commitment of real estate professionals to provide equal and fair treatment to all individuals in their professional activities. In addition, some states, and local jurisdictions, may have additional protected classes beyond those outlined in the Fair Housing Act, real estate professionals should also be up to date on these regulations to stay informed on how to best to serve Buyers and sellers in their cities and states.

Real estate professionals must ensure that they provide equal treatment to all Buyers. They must avoid comments about a Buyer's preferences or make assumptions about their lending or housing needs. They must also make sure that they do not steer Buyers to or away from certain neighborhoods based on stereotypes.

How should Fair Housing laws impact their marketing efforts?

A real estate professional should always make sure that their marketing efforts abide by fair housing laws. They must ensure that their advertisements and marketing materials do not contain any language or images that could be interpreted as discriminatory. This means avoiding any statements or pictures or videos that could imply a preference for or against individuals based on their characteristics. Additionally, they should strive to reach a diverse audience in their marketing campaigns to promote inclusivity and fair treatment for all potential Buyers. It is also important to use neutral language that welcomes all potential Buyers to properties and also when recruiting talent to the company.

Are there opportunities being overlooked regarding diversity fairness?

Yes, there are often opportunities being overlooked regarding diversity and fairness in the real estate industry. Real estate professionals can benefit from actively seeking out and serving diverse communities. This includes understanding the unique needs and preferences of different demographic groups and adapting their services to better meet those needs. Embracing diversity can lead to new business opportunities and foster a more inclusive and equitable real estate market. There are many organizations both locally and nationally that can help educate real estate professionals on how to serve today's diverse markets including organizations like the Asian Real Estate Association of America (AREAA), the National Association of Real Estate Brokers (NAREB), the National Association of Hispanic Real Estate Professionals (NAHREP), The LGBTQ+ Real Estate Alliance, the Women's Council of REALTORS® (WCR®), and the Veterans Association of Real Estate Professionals (VAREP.) Overall, these organizations play a crucial role in helping real estate professionals navigate today's diverse markets, stay informed about industry trends and best practices, and build relationships with clients from various backgrounds. By joining and participating in these organizations, real estate professionals can enhance their professionalism, expand their networks, and contribute to the promotion of diversity and inclusion in the real estate industry. In addition, real estate professionals can help advance sustainable homeownership in the communities that these organizations serve.

What are some examples that contributed to the need for Fair Housing laws?

There are so many examples that contributed to the need for fair housing laws including historical practices such as redlining, which systematically denied mortgages, insurance, and housing opportunities to minority groups in certain neighborhoods. Other examples include discriminatory lending practices, restrictive covenants, and outright refusal to sell or rent properties to individuals based on their race, religion, or other protected characteristics. These practices perpetuated segregation and inequality in housing markets, leading to the enactment of fair housing laws to combat such discrimination. Today, the enduring legacy of discriminatory housing practices continues to affect the homeownership rate for many minority communities. This disparity is a result of the historical denial of the opportunities mentioned above.

How do Fair Housing laws impact the use of social media?

Fair Housing Laws have a significant impact on the use of social media by real estate professionals. They must ensure that their social media posts, advertisements, and interactions comply with fair housing regulations. This means refraining from making any statements or taking any actions that could be perceived as discriminatory towards protected classes. Additionally, real estate professionals should be cautious when targeting specific demographics on social media to avoid unintentional discrimination. They should also be mindful to advertise properties based on location, or property type, not demographics.

Social platforms like Facebook have faced scrutiny for allowing advertisers to target or exclude certain demographics, leading to increased awareness and enforcement of fair housing laws in online advertising. Real estate companies have also faced heavy fines by marketing via social media their minimum home price policies which also were found to be discriminating against sellers and Buyers of homes in communities of color.

It is important that marketing professionals who work with real estate organizations take courses on fair housing so that they understand the law to avoid fair housing violations so that they can better represent the agents and the communities they serve.

As a Buyer Agent, how do I ensure that Clients understand how I can best represent them in a transaction?

Begin by arranging an initial consultation with your clients to delve into their home needs, desires, and goals, alongside their schedule, financial boundaries, and any constraints they may have. It's advantageous to utilize a comprehensive needs analysis form, ensuring consistency across all clients and facilitating your guidance throughout the process.

During this consultation, it's imperative to review fair housing laws with your clients, elucidating how you can best advocate for them. These laws, which prohibit discrimination based on various factors such as race, color, religion, and more, serve as the cornerstone of a just and equitable home-buying experience. As a Buyer's Agent, it's essential to treat all clients with parity, adhering to "The Equal Professional Service Model" established by the National Association of REALTORS®.

This model emphasizes employing systematic procedures, gathering objective information, allowing clients to set parameters, presenting diverse options, and meticulously documenting provided services.

If you implement prequalification requirements for your clients before property viewings, a common practice, it's vital to ensure consistency by mandating prequalification letters from all clients. This safeguards against potential liability under fair housing laws. Moreover, refrain from offering opinions on school quality, crime rates, or the demographic composition of neighborhoods to avoid the risk of steering.

By adhering to these principles and practices, you uphold fair housing standards, foster equitable treatment, and mitigate legal risks in your role as a Buyer's Agent. I would also like to salute Gary Acosta, the co-founder of NAHREP, and Charlie Oppler, past president of NAR, for their epic leadership regarding Fair Housing.

Should you have any additional questions regarding Fair Housing Law and real estate, free to connect with Teresa at TeresaSmith@homeservices.com

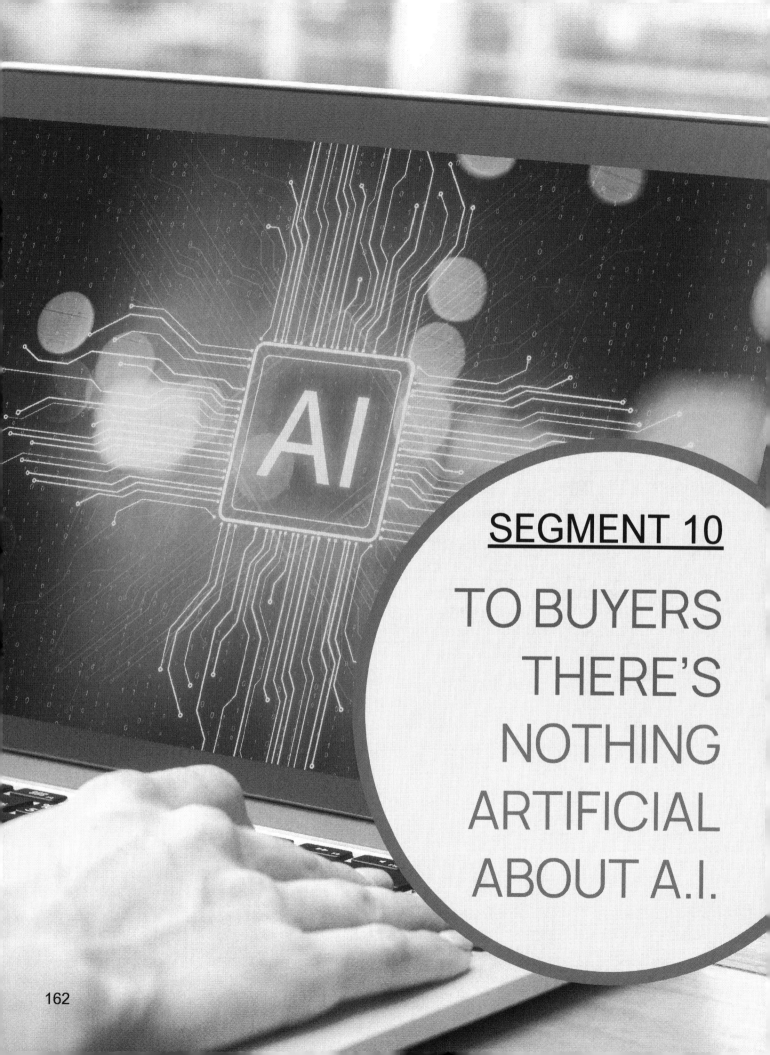

SEGMENT 10

TO BUYERS THERE'S NOTHING ARTIFICIAL ABOUT A.I.

Over the past few decades and during each advent of new technology that carries with its application to real estate, the real estate industry has gone through the intellectual process of trying to determine, "Will this latest innovation be our friend or foe?" Unquestionably, the first reaction always directs itself to the negative. When the internet first came over the horizon it was characterized as a "lion coming over the hill that would devour the industry" but it didn't. Then with IDX there was considerable early-on resistance. In retrospect, innumerable far-fetched fantasies that were ruminating over the perils of enabling Buyers to see all inventory on all real estate company websites were unfounded. Now with Artificial Intelligence, here again, there exists considerable consternation but this time the fear and anxiety extend well beyond the confines of the real estate industry. A question I have is, "To what degree will artificial intelligence empower Buyers to where they believe the information they require about communities, homes, services, school systems, climate, crime reports, etc., or facilitating a transaction they can derive from AI? Also, to what degree does this potential belief minimize how much money Buyers think they should pay for representation?"

My other question is, "How prepared are most real estate agents to ensure that at least, over the next several years, artificial intelligence becomes a tool of theirs versus them becoming an unwitting tool of AI?"

Now I have some questions/discussion points for each of you:

Do you see artificial intelligence as either a threat or a positive tool, especially when seeking or serving Buyers?

YES   or   NO

Do you know the difference between machine and deep learning?

YES or NO

Do you know the difference between generative AI and Predictive AI?

YES or NO

Do you have an AI presentation for Buyers?

YES or NO

Do you know how other professionals are using AI?

YES or NO

Do you know the difference between high tech and prop tech?

YES or NO

Have you decided on potentially how much artificial intelligence helps the Buyer the seller and your career?

YES or NO

In this segment you will be provided with some basic cursory answers and then some concluding questions and summary:

First an acknowledgment: The scope and scale of artificial intelligence is so vast and ever-changing that even if this entire consulting project was dedicated to artificial intelligence it would be inadequate, never mind this one brief segment within this buying side repor so vast and ever-changing that even if this entire consulting project was dedicated to artificial intelligence it would be inadequate, never mind this one brief segment within this buying side report.t.

Factors to consider:

1) Artificial intelligence (albeit some scientists predict the ultimate annihilation of the human species) should be viewed as an "invaluable" tool for real estate professionals.

2) The difference between machine and deep learning artificial intelligence is that machine learning harnesses historical data and can make predictions based on that data. It is more simple and less accurate than deep learning.

Deep learning does a better job of extrapolating data, through its ANN (artificial neuron network) which consists of layered information. This means that these layers sequentially process and learn from the preceding layer. Presumably, no Buyers (for now) will be asking, "Hey, did the forecasting you showed us come from machine learning or deeper learning?" but this is a subject and a distinction that you are encouraged to further explore. You can go to ChatGPT and ask, "Which form of artificial intelligence is more reliable when doing a CMA?"

3) Generative AI (as you know: ChatGPT) created text, audio, and video can help agents save enormous ideation time by creating both short and long-form content.

4) Predictive AI is where databases are algorithmically accessed in order to forecast, conduct predictive analysis, and recognize consumer buying patterns.

Question:
List examples of how you use generative AI to reach and serve Buyers.

_____   _____

_____   _____

_____   _____

List examples of how you use predictive AI to serve Buyers:

_____   _____

_____   _____

_____   _____

4) Do you have an AI presentation for Buyers?

YES or NO

Here is a recommended AI presentation for sellers:

"Folks, I provide my clients with three-dimensional lifestyle storytelling.

A) The first dimension is where I gain all of your most relevant and important insights as the first part of our lifestyle story.

B) Secondly, I use language models like ChatGPT regarding which words and amenities are most important to Buyers
Specifically within this price range and then look for authentic matches with your lifestyle.

C) Thirdly, I tap into my deep experiential knowledge along with my love of your property and community and integrate all three interrelated sources into as I say a three-dimensional lifestyle narrative or lifestyle story ...how does that sound?"

Reason:

Since you are not going to get into all of the immense power and usages of AI, you will need to show the homesellers that you have a human algorithm-like ability to synthesize three dimensions of lifestyle knowledge, which, while including harnessing and employing AI, also celebrates the human knowledge and emotion of both the home sellers and yourself.

A recommended Buyer presentation that involves artificial intelligence

Buyer presentation (just one suggestion) –

" folks I employ artificial intelligence in two major ways as a service to my Buyer clients

I will be using predictive artificial intelligence to help with pricing negotiations, community trends, Buyer matching through advanced property search technology, and virtual tours with 3-D visualization which will help us refine our potential homes virtually and also help you reimagine space usage. Artificial intelligence will also help in making the best mortgage recommendations and will help in the digital administration of any potential contract processes. We can also ask artificial intelligence what it thinks are reasons for and against buying a certain home, as well as the neighborhood or community.

This is something a seller's agent would never do because they represent the homesellers while I represent you (where applicable).

RITA REALBY
Real Estate Advisor

BUYERS!

Because I represent you and NOT the home sellers of the properties you are looking at (with some exceptions), I provide you and my other Buyer clients with AI reasons to consider buying (and not buying) homes ... and reasons to consider moving to (or not moving to) certain communities.

It's all part of being a
Trusted Real Estate Advisor!

Why should you buy XYZ Property, Fairfield CT

Here's some information to help you decide whether XYZ Property in Fairfield, CT is a good fit for you, without directly saying you should buy it:

- **Large and historic:** Public records indicate it's a sizable residence exceeding 6,000 square feet, built in 1897 [various real estate sites]. This could be attractive if you need a lot of space or enjoy a historic property.expand_more
- **Previously sold:** While there's no current listing available, it was sold in 2017 according to several real estate sites.expand_more This may give you leverage in negotiations if you pursue a similar purchase.
- **Desirable area:** Fairfield consistently ranks high in "best places to live" lists.expand_more This suggests a good quality of life and potentially strong resale value.expand_more

Here are some things to consider to help you decide:

- **Price:** The prior sale price of $2.1 million in 2017 may not reflect the current market value. It would be wise to get a proper valuation done.
- **Condition:** The details available online are from 1999.expand_more You'd want a thorough inspection to understand any renovations or updates needed.
- **Your needs:** With a large house, consider ongoing maintenance costs and if the layout suits your lifestyle.

I recommend reaching out to a realtor familiar with the area for a more detailed assessment of XYZ Property and its suitability for you.

Why should you NOT buy XYZ Property, Fairfield CT

While XYZ Property sounds impressive on paper, here are some reasons why it might not be the perfect fit:

- **Potentially outdated:** The descriptions online reference renovations in 1999. Depending on your preferences, the house might require modernization to match contemporary styles and amenities.
- **Maintenance costs:** A large, historic property likely has significant upkeep expenses. Consider factors like heating/cooling a large space, potential repairs for an older structure, and maintaining the extensive grounds.
- **Hidden issues:** The lack of recent updates on the property's condition could indicate potential problems. A thorough inspection is crucial to uncover unseen issues that could translate to hefty repair costs.
- **Unknown reason for off-market status:** It's unclear why the property is no longer actively listed. There could be reasons unrelated to the house itself, but it's worth investigating.

Additional considerations:
- **Property taxes:** Fairfield has high property taxes. Factor this into your budget calculations.
- **Privacy concerns:** The description mentions a "secret door." While intriguing, it could raise questions about the overall security of the property.
- **Needs assessment:** Carefully evaluate your needs and lifestyle. Do you require all that space? Is the layout functional for you?

Ultimately, the decision depends on your priorities and budget. Weigh the potential drawbacks against the property's strengths to determine if XYZ Property aligns with your vision for your next home.

Then I will use generators of artificial intelligence through geo-targeting neighborhoods and homes that you may be interested in that are not on the market .

SAMPLE REPORT

Why you should move to Fairfield CT

Fairfield, CT offers a lot to consider if you're looking for a new place to live. Here are some reasons why it might be a good fit:

Classic New England Charm:
- Beautiful Beaches: Fairfield boasts stunning beaches like Jennings Beach, perfect for swimming, sunbathing, and enjoying water sports [5].
- Historic Vibe: The town has a rich history with a charming downtown area offering a glimpse into the past [1].

Strong Community and Amenities:
- Top-Rated Schools: Fairfield boasts excellent public schools, a major draw for families [1].
- Active Community: With a variety of events and organizations, Fairfield offers opportunities to connect with others who share your interests [1].
- Convenient Location: Fairfield sits near I-95 and the Merritt Parkway, offering easy access to New York City and other destinations [2]. It also has Metro-North train stations for a convenient commute [2].

Nature and Outdoor Activities:
- Scenic Beauty: Fairfield offers stunning views of Long Island Sound and plenty of green spaces for nature lovers [3].
- Parks and Recreation: There are numerous parks with trails, playgrounds, and picnic areas for outdoor enjoyment [3].

Things to Keep in Mind:
- Cost of Living: Fairfield has a high cost of living, including expensive housing [1]. Consider your budget before making a decision.
- Small-Town Feel: Fairfield offers a charming, close-knit community feel, which may not suit everyone.

Overall, Fairfield is a great place to live for those who value beautiful surroundings, a strong sense of community, excellent schools, and easy access to amenities. However, it's important to weigh the cost of living and small-town atmosphere to see if it aligns with your priorities.

Why you should NOT move to Fairfield CT

Fairfield, CT might not be the perfect fit for everyone. Here's a look at some potential drawbacks to consider:

- High Cost of Living: Fairfield consistently ranks high for expensive housing and overall cost of living [1, 2]. Property taxes are high, and everyday expenses can add up quickly.
- Competitive Environment: Due to the excellent schools and desirable location, Fairfield can be a competitive place to live. Housing can move quickly, and there might be a competitive edge for spots in schools and activities.
- Limited Diversity: Fairfield leans towards a specific demographic. If you crave a more diverse community, you might find Fairfield lacking in that aspect.
- Potential for Traffic: While Fairfield itself might be charming, commuting can be another story. Traffic congestion, especially during rush hour on I-95 and the Merritt Parkway, can be a significant factor [2].

Additionally, consider these aspects:
- Small-Town Vibe: Fairfield offers a close-knit community feel, which can be great, but might feel stifling to those who prefer a more bustling environment.
- Limited Nightlife: Nightlife options in Fairfield might be limited compared to more urban areas.
- Seasonal Factors: Winters in Fairfield can be cold and snowy, with some residents finding the long winters a drawback.

Ultimately, the decision depends on your lifestyle and priorities. If affordability, a highly diverse environment, or a vibrant nightlife scene are high on your list, Fairfield might not be the ideal choice. However, for those seeking a beautiful, safe community with excellent schools and a strong focus on families, Fairfield offers a lot to consider.

5) How are other professionals using AI:

Doctors are using AI research and surgical procedures – specifically for intra-operative assistance/guidance and execution through robotic surgery.

Pilots are beginning to view AI as an additional co-pilot as machine learning provides simplified flight searches, more sustainable flights, and (for consumers) more competitive pricing.

Many Attorneys view AI as a "liberator" freeing them from tedious and, in many cases, nonbillable casework. AI helps to analyze large-scale data and document summarization.

Cautionary note: several federal judges have ruled that when artificial intelligence is used it must be revealed and caution against AI "hallucination" – this is where artificial intelligence has "invented" precedent examples.

That there will soon be legislation against improper or undisclosed use of AI-generated data and findings is **great news for real estate professionals.**

6) What do you think is the difference between high tech and prop tech?

The names high tech and high touch themselves are instructive. "High tech" is a general way of referring to all present and evolving transformational technology while "prop-tech" refers to technology that is employed in service of all digital aspects in the real estate continuum and experience.

"Fin-tech" would be the same when it comes to technology that applies to the financial industry and financial clients and consumers.

The reason this distinction is important is that it highlights that real estate, parenthetically, has now attracted technology findings designed expressly for commercial and residential real estate analytics and transactional processes. This is one of the reasons that the symmetry of "high tech" versus "high touch" is no longer in favor as it would now be a case of "prop-tech" versus "prop touch" (yours truly owns the URL prop touch). There are more than 2200 companies specializing in prop-tech and yet less than one-third of those companies say they have developed a "prop-touch" strategy.

Please answer **yes or no** if you are familiar with the following prop-tech deliverables and also if you use them:

1) Virtual reality and augmented reality –

This prop tech offering provides real estate Buyers with a new way to view real estate for sale. Augmented reality allows Buyers to see what a home could look like due to the ability to overlay computer-generated imagery.

Familiar?   Yes   No   •   Utilize?   Yes   No

2) CRM –

CRM stands for **Customer Relationship Management**. It is both, a type of strategy and a type of software. In simple words, CRM Strategy defines how your business builds and manages relationships with its customers.

Familiar?   Yes   No   •   Utilize?   Yes   No

3) Big Data – Big Data allows Buyers to optimize living spaces by utilizing predictive analytics.

Familiar?   Yes   No   •   Utilize?   Yes   No

4. Blockchain –

A blockchain stores data that cannot be altered after it is uploaded. All records become part of an open ledger and are immutable and always accessible.

Familiar?   Yes   No   •   Utilize?   Yes   No

5) IoT (internet of things) –

This prop tech innovation allows property owners to easily track who is visiting or entering the property.

Familiar?   Yes   No   •   Utilize?   Yes   No

6) Smartphone access –

Smartphone-powered access to homes provides many benefits for residents and guests.

Familiar?   Yes   No   •   Utilize?   Yes   No

7) Spacio – Digital open house lead gen

Familiar?   Yes   No   •   Utilize?   Yes   No

8) Canva – Online graphic design tool

Familiar?   Yes   No   •   Utilize?   Yes   No

9) Matterport – Real estate video marketing

Familiar?   Yes   No   •   Utilize?   Yes   No

10) BombBomb – Send video emails to prospects and more

Familiar?   Yes   No   •   Utilize?   Yes   No

11) Real Grader – Rate and enhance your social media

Familiar?   Yes   No   •   Utilize?   Yes   No

12) DocuSign – Digital document signing software that you can use to legally —and securely—collect approvals online in minutes

Familiar?   Yes   No   •   Utilize?   Yes   No

13) Google Drive – Easily share documents

Familiar?   Yes   No   •   Utilize?   Yes   No

14) MyNHD – Natural home disaster reports

Familiar?   Yes   No   •   Utilize?   Yes   No

15) Soci – Social media management

Familiar?   Yes   No   •   Utilize?   Yes   No

16) Chalk Digital – Allows you to geo-target and geo-fence specific areas for both prospecting sellers and Buyers and marketing for sellers and educating Buyers.

Familiar?   Yes   No   •   Utilize?   Yes   No

17) Zillow, Realtor.com, Homes.com, etc.

Familiar?   Yes   No   •   Utilize?   Yes   No

Please add any other real estate-specific technology you utilize:

_____   _____

_____   _____

_____   _____

Review all services on the list and select:

A) The category of technology you are presently using (regardless of brand or vendor).

B) Technology that you will now consider adding that you may not have before.

Below are ChatGPT results to basic prompts:

"What is the impact of AI on buying real estate?"

AI has had a significant impact on the real estate industry, particularly in the process of buying properties. Here are several ways AI influences this sector:

Data Analysis: AI algorithms can analyze vast amounts of data, including property prices, market trends, demographics, and even social media activity to provide insights into property value and investment potential. This helps Buyers make more informed decisions.

Predictive Analytics: AI-powered predictive analytics can forecast future trends in the real estate market, allowing Buyers to anticipate changes in property values and make timely purchases.

Virtual Tours and Imaging: AI technologies enable the creation of virtual tours and 3D imaging, providing potential Buyers with immersive experiences of properties without physically visiting them. This saves time and resources for both Buyers and sellers.

Personalized Recommendations: AI algorithms can analyze a Buyer's preferences, budget, and other factors to provide personalized property recommendations that match their criteria, streamlining the search process.

(cont.)

Risk Assessment: AI can assess risks associated with real estate investments by analyzing factors such as location, economic indicators, and historical data on property performance, helping Buyers make more informed decisions.

Automated Transactions: AI-powered platforms facilitate smoother and more efficient transactions by automating paperwork, contract processing, and other administrative tasks involved in buying real estate.

Chatbots and Customer Service: AI-driven chatbots can provide instant assistance to Buyers, answering questions, scheduling property viewings, and guiding them through the buying process, enhancing the overall customer experience.
Fraud Detection: AI algorithms can detect suspicious activities and patterns that may indicate fraudulent behavior in real estate transactions, enhancing security and trust in the buying process.

Overall, AI is revolutionizing the way people buy real estate by providing data-driven insights, enhancing convenience, and improving the efficiency and accuracy of transactions.

"How can real estate agents use AI when working with Buyers?"

Real estate agents can leverage AI in various ways to enhance their services when working with Buyers. Here are some ways AI can be beneficial:

Property Matching and Recommendation: AI algorithms can analyze vast amounts of data, including Buyer preferences, past behaviors, and market trends, to recommend properties that closely match the Buyer's criteria. This can save time for both agents and Buyers by narrowing down options to those most likely to meet the Buyer's needs.

Predictive Analytics: AI can help predict future trends in the real estate market, enabling agents to advise Buyers on potential investment opportunities or areas likely to see growth in property value. This insight can assist Buyers in making informed decisions about their purchases.

Virtual Tours and 3D Visualization: AI-powered virtual reality (VR) and augmented reality (AR) technologies can provide immersive virtual tours of properties, allowing Buyers to explore homes remotely and get a realistic sense of the space before scheduling physical visits. This can be particularly useful for Buyers who are relocating from a different city or country.

(cont.)

Natural Language Processing (NLP): AI-powered chatbots equipped with NLP capabilities can engage with Buyers, answer their questions, and provide information about properties in real time. These chatbots can operate on websites or messaging platforms, offering immediate assistance to Buyers at any time of the day.

Price Estimation and Negotiation Support: AI algorithms can analyze historical sales data, property features, and market conditions to estimate a fair price for a property. This information can empower agents to negotiate effectively on behalf of Buyers, ensuring they get the best deal possible.

Customer Relationship Management (CRM): AI-driven CRM systems can help agents manage their interactions with Buyers more efficiently by organizing contacts, scheduling follow-ups, and sending personalized communications based on Buyer preferences and behavior patterns.

Market Insights and Research: AI-powered tools can sift through large volumes of real estate market data, news articles, and social media discussions to provide agents and Buyers with valuable insights into local market conditions, upcoming developments, and neighborhood dynamics.

By incorporating AI into their workflow, real estate agents can streamline processes, provide personalized experiences to Buyers, and offer valuable insights that facilitate informed decision-making in the home buying process.

As you can see, this limited information reflects returns on two basic prompts and explains the need for the following :

1) You need to create many additional prompts

2) You need to access real estate thought leaders like Jimmy Burgess who not only teach the industry through Inman but are also involved in everyday brokerage.

DISCUSSION POINTS

1) Do you think the word artificial best describes this technology?

_____ _____
YES   NO

2) Do you think it will help real estate agents become either more valuable?

_____ _____
YES   NO

...less necessary

_____ _____
YES   NO

... less valuable?

_____ _____
YES   NO

3) What % of Buyers bring up the subject?

_____ %

4) Do you bring the subject up with Buyers?

_____ _____
YES   NO

5) Will AI help consumers find the best Home Service providers without you?

_____ _____
YES   NO

6) Who do you think can contribute more to the writing of a community video? You or AI?

_____ _____
ME   AI

7) Do you think consumers can detect when artificial intelligence is describing properties or communities?

_____ _____
YES   NO

8) What percentage of the text that you produce includes contributions from AI?

_____ %

9) Does AI help you more as a time saver or
a better communicator?
(Although it can be both choose one)

      _____   _____
      time   communication

10) List all the ways that you use AI now:

For Buyers: _____ _____

        _____ _____

For sellers: _____ _____

        _____ _____

For digital prospecting and personal
marketing:

        _____ _____

        _____ _____

Summary

As I have been known to say, "I may not be right but I am convinced," and specifically when I included in this book (which I am convinced no one has ever done or shown before) to use ChatGPT to criticize the properties and communities that you may show or negotiate on behalf of a Buyer, that some of our readers might be perplexed, perturbed, or cynical. "Allan, why would you ever try to be critical of a home or community you're trying to sell?" Simple. It suggests transparency, the Buyer Agent's job is not to praise the home or the community as much as the Seller Agent, it builds trust, and I have included this as an optional thing to do and say within The 7A's - realizing that 10% of Buyer Agents will absolutely go wild over this while 90% will never employ this approach. So there is no harm. If the Seller Agent uses A.I. to raise the price, then why can't a Buyer Agent discretely, respectfully, and sensitively use A.I. to lower the price?

NOTES

SEGMENT 11

CRM
MUST ALSO STAND FOR
CLIENT AND CONTENT
MANAGEMENT

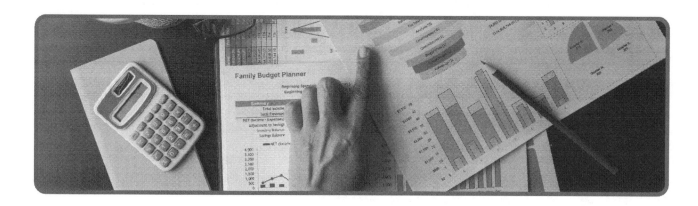

CRM – A Technological Gift for Increasing **Buyer-Side Value** and **Productivity**

"Be aware" that each segment within *BUYER AGENT BE AWARE* varies in length, and where some subjects are consolidated, for good reason.

Some subjects are presently so comprehensively and masterfully covered, and by those more knowledgeable than me, that I will merely share my personal recommendations and insights.

Even though the CRM Top Producer was one of my direct reports while serving as President of Move Inc., I have never paid significant attention to the many nuances of CRMs in general nor have I used one in my executive real estate roles during the last thirty years.

Yet here is what I will add to the subject. CRMs are more important to real estate professionals than the overwhelming majority of other business people or professionals and here is why:

A) Over 90% of employees or workers overall who work for companies "process work" and only 5 to 10% percent "create" work.

This means that if you were employed by most corporations or government agencies you would not be required to create your own business plan or select a CRM as these decisions would have been made for you.

B) In order to benefit, through the immense power and gifts of your CRM, you must generate enough confidence in your value and your long-range tenure in order to engage with potential Clients. This leads to creating contacts which in turn have to be followed up and ultimately managed before during and after transactions. Therefore, your CRM can be more motivational than any coach. A prerequisite of using a CRM is that you either need to have contacts and Clients or you must develop them... which requires confidence that you will follow up. This is why the number one question top agents across the industry have asked me for years is, "Allan, can you recommend a great CRM?"

C) Be aware that if you do not have a CRM that can manage and market to contacts, that this void alone automatically devalues the importance of every single person, prospect, or potential Client you will ever meet, for the rest of your "vulnerable" career. Especially now on the home seller side with the average length of homeowners not selling over ten to 12 years versus 7 to 8 in past years.

D) There is a great parallel between how a politician needs to keep in touch with constituents and how real estate professionals need to keep in touch with prospects and Clients. One of my friends went on to become the Mayor of Boston. He was known for how, in High School, he would keep a 3 x 5 card of everyone he ever met which listed their name, names of family members, pets, and interests. This activity was well before our days of technology-based CRMs. Yet it showed even back then the importance of systematically gathering and storing people-related information. Today fortunately all of these tasks, and many more, are done for you automatically through CRMs.

E) For years agents would say the following, "I know that personal websites have very little value regarding Buyer or seller search but I need to have one as it acts like a resume or, even more modestly, as an online business card. Therefore, when consumers or potential Clients get to the lower levels of the sales funnel they will see my resume."

Because of the integration of CRMs with personal websites, mobile phones, and social media platforms, websites have now become exponentially more important and elevated regarding the sales funnel. All lead gen, social media efforts, use of video powered by BombBomb, Chalk Digital, geo-targeting, drip marketing campaigns, etc. can and should link to your website.

F) This capability also applies justifiable pressure on top-producing agents to make sure that their websites go well beyond IDX listings and personal profiles. Instead, websites need to be converted into highly impressive citadels or cathedrals of consumer and Client-centric content.

G) Through the data and artificial intelligence capabilities of your CRM you can strategically provide market updates in certain categories of your demographics for first-time Buyers to investors and everyone in between.

H) You can wow consumers whose names you populate by reaching out to them and including all of their names. You can have text, emails, and even videos sent out when Buyers look multiple times at a property or, when they look at a different town, simply by employing a number of tags that your auto list will handle.

Now I am going to stop here on "functionality" as this whole report is not even big enough to list all of the ways that your CRM can function. Moreover, there is extensive training within the industry made available to you regarding CRM usage. What I will address are some additional thoughts and methods that I would like to contribute to how you perceive your CRM and how you process its operational value.

I typically hear real estate professionals, when discussing the concept of a CRM speaking in terms of its official name "Customer Relationship Management." Well, for those who know me and my work, I am sure you can anticipate my thoughts. **CRM should also represent for you "Client Relationship Management" and "Content Relationship Management".** Here is why I am so passionate about these distinctions. Most of the business world defines **"consumers" as "customers".** Businesses, however, serve **"customers"** while professions and professional practices serve **Clients".**

Regarding content:

1) If there were a "do not be contacted by a real estate agent registry" do you think a significant percentage of consumers would register? Perhaps ... yet consumers want content and, at times, much more than to be contacted!

2) We're in an age where institutions and conventional values are under attack.

3) These distinctions are not merely matters of semantics. Some of you may recall several years ago my pointing out the following, "If you refer to people as **Past Clients** you will treat them as **Past Clients** and you will be treated by them as a **Past agent**."

This is why even with CRMs in use over the last twenty years, "the Real Estate Loyalty Gap" (a term popularized by industry icon and former CEO of BHHS, Chris Stuart) has not changed... with 90 percent of Clients saying they will return to their agent while less than 12 percent actually do. Why so?

Because, in the Information Age, market data is abundantly available and therefore it is hard to sustain a relationship over ten years or to begin a relationship by merely **following up with someone with data**... although these activities are a must. Rather, contacts must be converted from databases to Client bases a.s.a.p. ... yet this requires content, knowledge, wisdom, and trusted advice. Essentially all CRMs still speak in terms of databases and Past Clients! Today's agents now enjoy the opportunity to form and redefine "databases" to "Client bases" by more strategically and skillfully optimizing CRM capabilities.

Questions/Discussion:

1. When do you think you can begin to refer to someone as your Client?

2. Do you think it can only be during a transaction?

3. Can it be after a transaction? Can it be before?

4. Can you automate a category of your CRM-generated and distributed emails, texts, and newsletters with a beginning such as "Dear Client"?

5 . What would happen if you sent a text to someone who asked you for real estate information as "Dear Client"?

6. What if all correspondence from you to so-called Past Clients came out from your CRM as "Dear Client"?

Additional questions/discussion:

1) Should you send out a link to your website or a flip book with your guides' information from your CRM? Who would you send to and Why?

2) Should you send out community testimonial surveys from your CRM?

3) Should you announce that you attended a convention or that you represented your city at a convention?

4) How about distributing focused information regarding moving for those with pets to everyone you've learned who has a pet (since 71% do) or should you just send this content to everyone in your database and Client base?

5) Should you send out through your database and BombBomb video invitations to your Buyers' seminar?

6) How about sending information about "when it is best to buy" to apartment buildings through your CRM and Chalk Digital?

7) For the luxury communities you have separated in your CRM, how about sending information about downsizing?

8) How about distributing information about "why homes might not sell" to your CRM list of all expireds?

9) How about distributing, through your CRM, a holiday-based home marketing guide to everyone beginning after Halloween and through the first of the year?

Discussion Topics:

1) Do you think a CRM should also stand for "Content and Client Management"?

2) Do you agree that most agents in most companies merely settle for generic approaches and content versus distinct brand or brokerage content?

3) Which content are you distributing? When and to whom? How do you measure results?

4) How much of your content is video?

5) How much of the responses you receive are from your listings versus non-property-related text and video content?

6) In the segment on open houses, it covered how to ensure you get proper names and information to load into your CRM. Do you routinely do this?

7) How much are you using your CRM to distribute market data? What types?

8) How many names do you have in your database? How many in your Client base?

9) How do you use your CRM to generate and distribute testimonials and reviews?

10) Is your CRM more useful in securing listings or Buyers?

11) What "drip" or marketing campaigns are you doing through your CRM?

12) Have you ever used your CRM to manage a development and attract new construction Buyers? (See segment on New Construction Buyers)

13) What are the most important ways that your CRM helps you to make transactions more efficient?

14) What are the three most important ways that you are using your CRM?

15) Do you believe it would be worthwhile to do the following:

a) Upgraded some of your database to your Client base?

b) Caused Clients to do real estate planning with you?

c) Sent a link to your home maintenance vendors?

d) Sent out content about renting versus buying, how to "move up", senior lifestyles, investment opportunities, ways to make a home more valuable, luxury-specific information, invitations to Buyers seminars, how to appeal property taxes, and community videos that will exponentially increase my Range, Reach, Influence, and Results?

YES   or   NO

Which Content will you begin to Distribute and When?

_____

_____

_____

_____

_____

NOTES

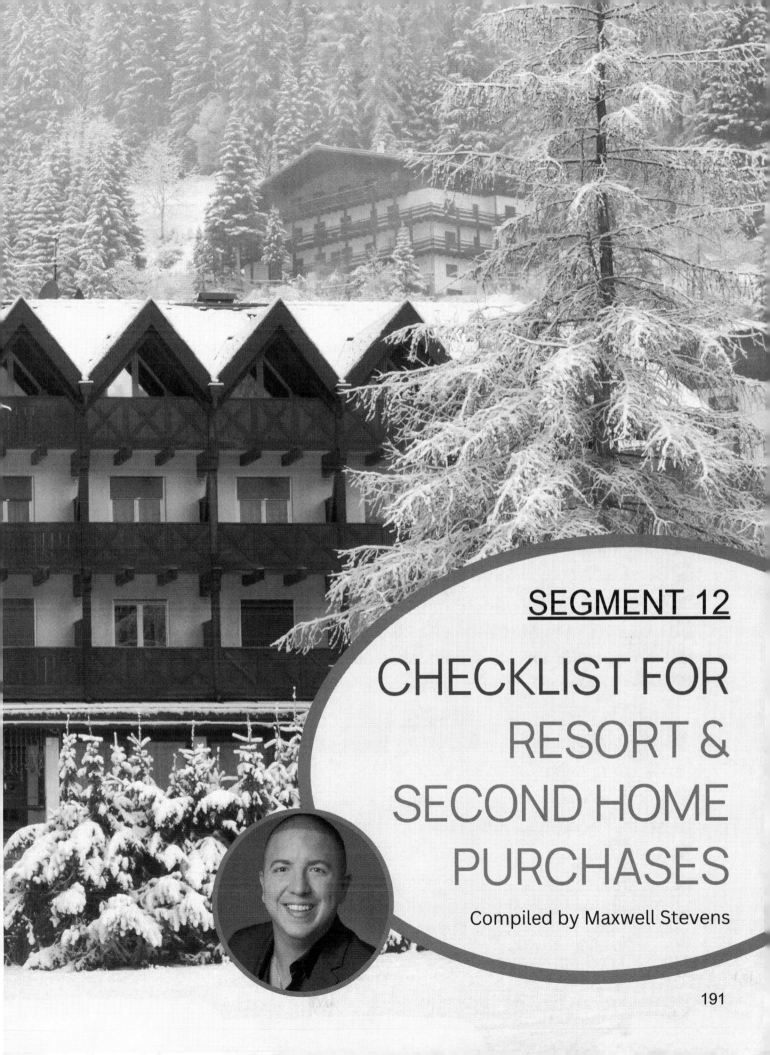

SEGMENT 12

CHECKLIST FOR RESORT & SECOND HOME PURCHASES

Compiled by Maxwell Stevens

A word about Maxwell Stevens:

Maxwell Stevens epitomizes both exemplary professionalism today as well as representing the best in real estate for the future. I asked Maxwell to cover what he and Buyers should discuss regarding Resort and Second Home purchasing and investing. You can read Maxwell's brief bio on the back on the book.

•···•

THE MAXWELL STEVENS HOME BUYER CHECKLIST FOR
A RESORT AND SECOND HOME PURCHASE

These are the areas of information that are **vital** in a successful property/lifestyle purchase:

- Knowledge of the specific communities and areas.
- What amenities are in each area?
- Rules and regulations of each community.
- If campers/boats are allowed to be parked in driveways.
- Can fencing be put up for pets?
- Townships and county knowledge
- Lakefront or waterfront rules and regulations.
- Powerboat & non-powerboat lakes available in the area.
- What activities and things to do in the area for each type of client adults, children, families, elderly
- Where hospitals are and how far they are from each home.
- Where healthcare facilities are
- Dentists, eye doctors, and other specialists in the area.
- Know if and what type of Internet access is available in each area.
- Know Airbnb rules and regulations for each area
- Know septic sizes for each home and if it's legal.
- Know the history of the area and how the homes were built.
- Know the depths of water and each lake's characteristics
- Know tax information

- Local zoning laws and regulations.
- Have good relationships with SEO and township supervisors.
- Market data. How many homes are on the market, those that have sold, Average sale price average days on the market, etc.
- Know where the best burger is in town.
- Have great relationships with local businesses
- Have great connections with local tradespeople
- Have great relationships with local lenders and banks
- Know school districts
- Know of local events that go on throughout the year
- Have good relationships with the marinas and outdoor shops in town.
- Have on-call electricians and plumbers available for emergency repairs.
- Be able to stop by homes to check in while clients are away.
- Have cleaning services for both investment properties short-term rentals and second homes.
- Know good reliable fair landscaping companies to help clients build their curb appeal.
- Be knowledgeable about what improvements help merchandise the property they are buying and help build value for potential resale.
- Where local golf courses and country clubs are and have good relationships with them.
- Concierge service and great relationships with the best restaurants to get people a table on busy nights while they are in town.
- Know where local event spaces are for weddings and celebrations.
- Know the best coffee shops

- Have great relationships with furniture & mattress stores.
- When seeing somebody at the supermarket, say hi listen and remember the small details of their life
- Have good relationships with other agents lenders and title companies.
- Have great relationships with inspectors.
- Have knowledge about tax benefits from investment properties and 1031 transactions.
- Have good relationships with photographers for clients to take Airbnb photos and market their property to the fullest after the sale.
- Know how to market short-term rental properties and what buyers should put into their properties to make sure they are getting good rental potential.
- Know where the local ski areas are and their difficulty level.
- Know local hiking trails and biking trails.
- Know public access to lakes.
- Know hunting regulations and where clients can hunt and where to get their hunting license.
- Know great fishing spots and where clients can get fishing licenses.
- Have good relationships with car mechanics so clients can have a safe ride home back to their primary residence
- Know of great deals on the market and after-repair value for investors who want to start flipping
- Know what local long-term rentals are renting for.
- Know where local vets and emergency veterinary clinics are.
- Have good relationships with local motorcycle and off-road vehicle dealers and service centers

- ■ Know of local daycares and where clients have access to child care.

- ■ Know and keep informed about what is coming to the area ie. new condos, and historical sites. Walking trails. Hotels and infrastructure

- ■ How will the home be maintained during winter or when the client isn't using the home

- ■ When do homes need to be winterized

- ■ When do docks need to be out of the water?

- ■ Help Clients keep track of capital improvements to the home to help with resale in the future and capital gains taxes. It's good to improve your home for value and taxes.

- ■ What types of mortgages are needed for second homes and investment homes?

The route to most of this is kindness and consideration. Greeting people with an earnest desire to help them. If you're number one goal is helping people it doesn't matter what the industry or the market is doing. There will always be opportunities.

Should you have any additional questions, feel free to connect with Maxwell at maxwell@poconorealestate.com

SEGMENT 13

BUYER KITS
AND PACKAGES
ARE NOT ENOUGH

I am assuming that most of the real estate professionals reading **BUYER AGENT BE AWARE** or discussing various segments of this publication with colleagues (or during training) have made the following comments with Sellers during a Listing/Marketing Presentation:

"I would like to review my marketing plan with you."

"Are you familiar with our company's marketing system?"

"I would like to review my '21 Point Listing Presentation' with you."

"I would like to review with you my Seller's Guarantee."

"I would like to tell you a little bit about myself, my company, and what we will do to sell your home."

"I want to help you get the best price in the shortest period of time with the least inconvenience."

"How are you going to select your agent?"

"Would you like to begin reviewing either pricing or marketing?"

"Most agents focus on selling more homes, my focus is on selling homes for more!"

How About What You Say to Buyers? I am assuming that far fewer agents have ever said this to a Buyer:

"I would like to review with you my Home Buying Plan?"

"I would like to review with you my Home Buying System."

"I would like to review with you my Buyer's Guarantee."

"I want to help you buy the right home with the least inconvenience at the lowest possible price."

"How are you going to select your buyer agent (which you shouldn't ask)?

"Most agents focus on selling more homes my focus is selling homes for less!"

These examples, **if the answers lead to greater preparation in communicating value to Home Sellers versus Home Buyers**, confirm and reinforce the obvious… that the real estate industry, in general, is infinitely better prepared to present and differentiate their value with Home Sellers than with Buyers.

The reasons why there has been exponentially greater industry-wide focus on how to make Listing or Marketing Presentations versus **Buyer Presentations** is quite explicable:

1) Because the overwhelming percentage of Buyers in North America have never either expected or had to directly pay a fee to the Buyer Agent

2) Perhaps because the industry's favorite chant has always been, "Listings are the name of the game," NOT, "Buyers are the name of the game!"

3) Listings create Buyers more than Buyers create Listings

4) Sellers look for the Agent first before marketing their home… whereas Buyers look for the properties first and then that takes them to the Buyer

5) Buyers do not expect a presentation, instead, a consultation (or merely a review of wants and needs) and then, off to the races!

In this section of **Buyer Agent Be Aware** I cover the importance of a Home Buying System. Please note that I did not say, "Home Buying Plan!"

Although I believe a company should create 'The Home Buying System' and indivisible agents should develop a 'Home Buying Plan' for each Buyer, let's start out by exploring **the difference between a Plan and a System!**

System: A group of interacting or interrelated elements that according to a set of rules helps form a unified plan.

Plan: A detailed proposal for doing or achieving something.

I encourage all of the companies I am now consulting to first create a System for the entire company and then their agents should create a plan for Buyer's Consultation and Presentations.

The reason why a 'Buyer Consultation' (an increasingly beloved term) is not enough… if it does not include a Presentation or Proposal… is as follows:

The role of a Consultant is to first determine needs, explore alternatives, and then leave it to the client (either with or without the Consultant) to make changes and implement solutions.

This is not enough because a Buyer Agent should already have (given the repetitive nature of how people buy homes) a reliable and systematic method of serving Buyers… which needs to be 'presented' over and above the fact-finding and rapport established through relevant questions **as part of a consultative process.**

Systems at the macro level trump systems:
Please forgive the analogy – Prisons create 'Systems' to retain Prisoners while Prisoners create 'Plans' to escape.

Which of the two is more successful and which of the two would people spend more money to acquire?

We want our automobiles, hopefully, to be equipped with anti-lock brake 'Systems' and not anti-lock 'plans'! This is why the saying, "The best-laid plans of mice and men," (which points out the significant uncertainty of plans) is not instead, "The best-laid Systems of mice and men!"

Broker owners and team leaders who possess marketing departments with digital expertise and accomplished writing and graphics: If you do not already have a specific 'Home Buying System' and instead (like most companies) merely have a 'Home Buyer's Guide ' or a 'Home Buyer's Packet' (etc.), consider creating your company or team's 'Home Buying System'.

By creating your company's Home Buying System, it signals that your organization (through the sharing of the collective expertise of your agents, your transactional and administrative and home-related services, and real estate ecosystems) has made a science out of the anatomy of a Home Buying Process. Moreover, that all buyers (regardless of which company agent serves them) receive fundamental value and services that have been tested and proven throughout your company and or brand. You might also want to build and announce your 'Customized Home Buying System'.

A Customized Home Buying System then enables all individual agents (who also require individual differentiation and to manifest personal creativity) to now **customize** and create a Customized Plan for each individual Buyer Client. As Buyers are increasingly going to be asked to pay a negotiated fee, then the more advanced leveraging of systems on the Buying-side, like the Marketing-side, is in order.

On the Marketing-side, value is expanded due to the focus provided to MLS, IDX, Open Houses, For Sale Signs, Videos, Brochures, Social Media, Luxury, etc. Comparable Buyer-side Systems now must be replicated and conveyed on the Buying-side in order to validate that Buying-side Value is also dependent on Systems and Services **versus what many Buyers might presently imagine.**

This is also why I have created the **7 A's of Buyer Agent Value** to also convey that there exists a highly organized methodical process... yet one which can be customized by individual agents, and where a System becomes a foundational benefactor of a subsequent Personalized Plan.

(Watch my 'homemade video')

Because I have seen Buyer's Guides, Buyer's Check Lists, and Buyer Folders, yet not 'Buying Systems' or organized and compelling 'Buyer Agent Value Presentations', I am sharing not only my recommended 'Buyer Presentation' but also an example of a Home Buying System I created over 35 years ago.

Now before you start laughing at how long ago this was or proclaim that this was, "Not digital," please hold off on your preconceptions and, instead, carefully review this organized display of buyer representation... and then determine how you would update and digitized this process.

Let's review this process together and see if it can help brokers and agents develop a deliverable that you can present physically to Buyers during your presentation and as a compelling 'Marketing and Social Media Content' offering. I am currently working with Clients, helping them to develop their private-labeled Home Buying System featuring my **7 A's of Buyer Agent Value**.

1. Make sure you and this deliverable feature (both digitally and physically on the front cover) your **Company Name** and **Home Buying System** for the reasons mentioned earlier.

(I can help if you need me)

Dear Reader,

I am pleased to present you with our **"Home Buying System"** booklet.

We at Murphy Realty/Better Homes and Gardens have learned through years of providing high caliber assistance to our clients that whether one is purchasing one's first home or is a multi-time buyer that there is an obvious need for counseling and assistance from a well-trained and caring real estate professional.

Individuals and families alike seek not only that "right home" but also the right "lifestyle."

In order for a real estate company and its representatives to respond to all of your home purchase needs, the services must include assistance that ranges from helping you to establish your housing needs through the conclusion of the home buying process, settling-in. In order for these services to be successful, they must be company-wide and systematized.

Our Home Buying System will help you and your Murphy representative establish a meaningful professional relationship as it will serve as a mutual frame of reference regarding the fundamentals relative to purchasing property.

We realize that just as no two moves are alike, no two peoples' needs are alike. All Murphy people are committed to working diligently and creatively to see that your unique needs are met.

As a member of many metropolitan area Multiple Listing Systems, we have access to virtually every property for sale in the region, regardless of which company has it listed and we endeavor to do everything possible to help you find your right home.

Thank you for the confidence you have placed in us and congratulations on being able to make this area your home. You'll love it!

Respectfully,

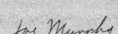

2) Create a Cover Letter from the CEO or Leader, remember this is a system for the entire company!

(Check out the tone and appeal of the message... perhaps prompt ChatGPT to see if A.I. can do better... I doubt it!)

3) The next page determines needs wants and desires. Acknowledges an appreciation of the three dimensions of home-buying motivation.

Determining Your Needs, Wants and Desires

We at Murphy Realty/Better Homes and Gardens suggest you start the home buying process by determining the type of housing which will best suit your desired lifestyle.

In determining your desired lifestyle, some of the questions you might want to consider are:

- Are you looking for a new home or a resale?
- How many bedrooms do you need?
- Do you want an inground pool?
- Do you want a large piece of property?
- How important is privacy?
- Is a condo or co-op right for you?
- Are you looking for a family-oriented neighborhood?

While deciding what type of housing best suits your lifestyle, we encourage you to communicate your needs and desires to your Murphy Sales Executive. He or she will note and discuss with you exactly what your preferences are. The more information we have to work with the easier it will be to find the home and lifestyle you seek.

In addition to the Buyers Needs Analysis form, your Murphy Sales Executive is prepared to supply you with the necessary demographic information to help to put in perspective your selection of homes, neighborhoods, school systems, community activities and transportation.

Some of the factors to be considered when selecting an area are:

- Does the area offer recreational facilities?
- How close is public transportation?
- Do the area's educational facilities meet your standards?
- What are the commutation costs and methods of transportation?
- Are necessary services and shopping convenient?

4) The next page represents a montage of Hone Architectural Styles designed to provide helpful and evocative renderings of lifestyle options.

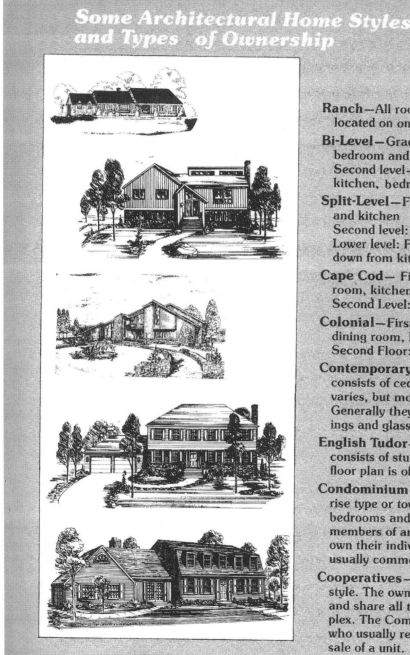

Some Architectural Home Styles and Types of Ownership

Ranch—All rooms, including bedrooms, are located on one floor.

Bi-Level—Grade level family room and possibly a bedroom and bath. Garage
Second level—Living room, dining room, kitchen, bedrooms, bath(s)

Split-Level—First level: Living room, dining room and kitchen
Second level: Bedrooms
Lower level: Family room located a few steps down from kitchen.

Cape Cod— First Level: Living room, dining room, kitchen, usually 2 bedrooms and bath. Second Level: 2 bedrooms

Colonial—First Floor: Entry hall, living room, dining room, kitchen.
Second Floor: Bedrooms and baths.

Contemporary—The exterior most commonly consists of cedar or red wood. The floor plan varies, but most are similar to a colonial. Generally they feature openness, cathedral ceilings and glass.

English Tudor—The exterior most commonly consists of stucco and wood trim. The interior floor plan is often similar to a colonial.

Condominium—The buildings are either high rise type or townhouse style. The number of bedrooms and bath vary. Homeowners are members of an association. The homeowners own their individual units and the grounds are usually common areas.

Cooperatives—Generally apartment building style. The owners own the building collectively and share all the expenses to maintain the complex. The Complex is run by a board of directors who usually require approval in the event of a sale of a unit.

5) The next page covers the **Mortgage and Finance Process**. For those companies with mortgage companies of preferred relationships, this is something you can do for all of your agents which helps them to better demonstrate the **'Sixth A'** – Administering the Transactions (again this is why this is a 'Home Buying System'!)

Exploring Your Financial and Mortgage Options

Most of today's property purchases require a mortgage. Your Murphy Sales Executive is prepared and highly trained to help you determine the type and amount of mortgage you need based on your own personal situation.

When you determine the amount of initial investment you want to make on your new home, also take into consideration closing costs which include loan origination fees, points, title search, survey and attorneys' fees.

Generally a lender will use 28% / 36% of your gross monthly income as a guideline for mortgage qualifying. This means that your principal, interest, taxes and insurance (PITI), considering you have no monthly debts, should not exceed 28% of your gross monthly income. Additionally PITI and monthly debts (i.e., car loan, charge cards, child support, etc.) should not exceed 36% of your gross monthly income.

If you need an equity advance, ask about our HELP (Home Equity Leverage Program).

Should you place less than 20% down you will be required to pay premium mortgage insurance (PMI), which is a monthly charge added to your mortgage payment. PMI is insurance which protects the lender.

6) The Value of Working Together. This page validates the Value of Arranging a showing and getting Access – two of the seven A's.

The Value of Working Together

Your Murphy Sales Executive will be working diligently for you, on a daily basis, in order to find the property you are looking for.

He or she will check every listing and lead available, whether the home is listed with Murphy Realty / Better Homes and Gardens or with another real estate company. Your Murphy Sales Executive will work very hard with you, because by working together you will be able to achieve results more effectively. There is no substitute for teamwork.

There is no substitute for teamwork.

7) The next page is about Selecting the Right Property

Selecting the Right Property

Once you have calculated how much you wish to spend and the type of area and home you would like, it's time to start the home search process.

Murphy Sales Executives are distinguished by how well acquainted they are with the communities, neighborhoods and the homes they present. Murphy Realty / Better Homes and Gardens is a member of all northern New Jersey Multiple Listing Services, offering access to homes in a variety of neighborhoods, styles and price ranges. Murphy Sales Executives continuously preview these MLS homes to be aware of current real estate inventory.

As part of Murphy's Home Buying System, you will be provided with a map of the areas you will be touring and a Home Evaluation Booklet, in which you can make notes and evaluate the individual properties you see.

While previewing the homes with your Murphy Sales Executive, be ready to evaluate those of interest to you.

- Notice the overall condition of each home, including the roof and exterior.
- Make note of the condition of the interior of the house and inspect the kitchen appliances.
- Examine the bathroom tiles for looseness and caulking.

The engineer who inspects the property will review these points in a physical inspection report later. Few homes are in perfect move-in condition. There is always a certain amount of wear and tear in resale homes, but your personal touch can not only improve the looks of the home but its overall condition.

A few of many considerations that buyers have are:

- What is the size of the property?
- What is included in the purchase price?
- Is there a septic tank or is there a city sewer system?
- Is there adequate street lighting?
- Are the other homes in the neighborhood well maintained?

8) The next page is about The Purchasing Process...

The Purchasing Process

Once you have found the home you want to purchase, our aim is to see that the home you desire becomes a reality. How do we do that?

You and your Murphy Sales Executive will prepare a purchase agreement which will include all the terms and conditions of the real estate transaction. New Jersey law requires all contracts for the sale of real estate to be in writing.

You will want to review these elements found in a real estate contract:

1. Mutual acceptance—"Meeting of the Minds" There is a willingness for both parties to enter into a contract.

2. Legally competent parties—For a contract to be legally enforceable parties of the contract must be of sound mind and of legal capacity. Minors, mental defectives and intoxicated persons do not have full contractural capacity.

3. Consideration—Earnest money deposit accompanies an "offer to purchase" agreement. When the offer is accepted, the money is applied to the purchase price.

4. Legal purpose—to be enforceable, a contract cannot have any illegal connotations. Contracts contrary to good moral and general public policy are also unenforceable.

5. Description of Property—The address of the property, lot and blocknumber are to be included in the contract.

6. Attorney Review—By law, all New Jersey real estate contracts are subject to a three-day attorney review period (see Working With Your Attorney and New Jersey Law for details).

7. Signatures of Parties—Once the contract is signed and delivered to all parties it is considered a legally binding contract. In the event one party is out of the area and cannot be present to sign the contract, a telegram can be sent verifying the acceptance of the contract. The telegram should highlight all important points agreed upon. For example, purchase price, closing date, any contingencies.

PHYSICAL INSPECTION
TERMITE INSPECTION

THIS CONTRACT IS WRITTEN IN PLAIN LANGUAGE. IF YOU HAVE ANY QUESTIONS YOU SHOULD CONSULT YOUR ATTORNEY

REALTOR®

Murphy Realty / Better Homes and Gardens

"THIS IS A LEGALLY BINDING CONTRACT THAT WILL BECOME FINAL WITHIN THREE BUSINESS DAYS. DURING THIS PERIOD YOU MAY CHOOSE TO CONSULT AN ATTORNEY WHO CAN REVIEW AND CANCEL THE CONTRACT. SEE SECTION ON ATTORNEY REVIEW FOR DETAILS."

CONTRACT OF SALE

1. PURCHASE: AGREEMENT AND PROPERTY DESCRIPTION   Dated _____, 19___

purchase from _____ Purchaser, agrees to through the REALTOR(S) named in this Agreement at the price and terms as stated below, the following Property

Property Address _____ Seller.

8. Balance of 10% monies—in order for a seller to feel secure in taking the house off the market, the attorney for the seller will advise his client to take at least a 10% deposit which will be kept in escrow until time of closing.

9. Financing contingenicies—The agreement is usually contingent upon the purchaser's obtaining financing. The normal period given to obtain a mortgage is 45 days from the date of the contract.

10. Closing date—The agreement will include the date and place of the closing. Usually the closing will take place at one of the attorneys' offices or at the office of the Realtor. The closing is expected to take place on or before the date mentioned in the contract.

11. Items included and excluded—in order to insure that there is no misunderstanding on what is included in the sale, your agent will discuss inclusions during the initial negotiations with the seller.

Additional contractural provisions refer to the physical inspection, termite inspection and flood plain verification (see Home Inspections).

Once the offer to purchase is prepared, your agent will present the offer to the seller or seller's representative. After he or she has reviewed the terms and conditions of the agreement, the seller will have three options:

1. Accept the offer by signing the agreement.
2. Make a counter-offer on one or more of the conditions
3. Reject the offer completely.

9) The next page is about working with either Attorneys or Escrow Companies...

Working with Your Attorney and New Jersey Law

Editor's note: Northern New Jersey attorneys have earned the respect of Murphy Realty / Better Homes and Gardens and the entire real estate community and we are proud of the fine job that they do and the important role they play in successful real estate transactions.

Your attorney will play an integral part in the real estate transaction. One of the first things you will want to do during the home-buying process is to enlist the services of a real estate attorney. Why a real estate attorney? An attorney who does not routinely participate in real estate transactions may be less familiar with ongoing changes in local zoning and building regulations, federal regulations pertaining to real estate transfers, and mortgage financing and availability.

The offer to purchase will be subject to a three-day attorney review once it is fully executed. The three-day period refers to three business days—weekends and holidays are excluded.

Using his or her legal expertise, your attorney will examine the contract. With your best interests in mind, he will make any necessary changes or suggestions. If there are changes to be made to the contract he will notify the seller's attorney of the changes within the three-day period.

By law, either attorney, whether she be the buyer's or sellers' representative, has the right to reject the contract for any reason, even if the price is the motivating factor.

Your attorney may also be able to help you arrange financing. An active real estate attorney will be familiar with the various local banks and mortgage companies. In addition to your real estate representative, your attorney can often help you find the best mortgage package for you.

While the mortgage is being processed, your attorney will make arrangements for the title to be searched and the property to be surveyed.

- Title Search—the purpose of a title search is to research all recorded documents which may effect the title of the property. Documents that may effect the title include: easements, mortgages, wills, judgments, pending law suits, marriages and divorces. The title search is performed to protect the buyer's interests and to obtain clear title to the property at the time of closing.
- Survey—every parcel of land which becomes part of a sale must be properly identified or described through a survey done by a civil engineer

Home Inspections

At Murphy, we advise all our purchasers to have a termite and physical inspection performed. In most cases, the offer to purchase agreement will be contingent upon the purchaser's obtaining a satisfactory physical inspection and termite inspection report. The contracts usually require the inspections to take place within 7 to 10 days of the signing and delivery of the contracts.

Physical Inspection

The purpose of a physical inspection is to inform the purchaser of the physical structure of the home. The inspector will often bring to the purchaser's attention methods which can be used to maintain the home.

Termite Inspection

A reputable termite company should be employed to make a thorough inspection of the interior and exterior of the property. Many banks and mortgage companies require a termite certification.

The Final Inspection

We encourage you to inspect the property prior to closing. Your agent will make arrangements for you to do so. The purpose of the walk-through is to satisfy you that the property is in the same condition as at the time of purchase with the exception of normal wear and tear.

Flood Plain Inspection

If the property you're considering presents any evidence of wetness or is in a tidal plain your attorney can procure a Flood Plain Verification certificate for you.

11) The next page explains the Closing Process...

The Closing

Once the mortgage commitment is secured and your attorney has prepared all the necessary paper work and completed the title search and survey, a closing can take place.

Some of the required documents that you and your attorney will need for a closing are: The Agreement of Sale, the Deed, The Abstract of Title, Insurance Policies, Mortgage Documents, a survey of the property and RESPA or closing statement.

You will need to bring a Homeowners Insurance policy to the closing. Your Murphy Sales Executive would be happy to refer you to the Murphy Insurance Company for assistance.

THINGS TO BE DONE PRIOR TO CLOSING

Make arrangements for the final inspection of the property with your agent.

Contact utility companies to transfer services.

Obtain Homeowners Insurance Policy.

Select a moving company.

WHAT TO BRING TO THE CLOSING

Bring your check book.

Call your attorney to see if a Certified check is needed.

Bring a folder to hold all important documents you will receive.

*Murphy Insurance 201-930-1170

12) The next page reveals the 'Seventh A' – After the Sale or Closing.

AFTER THE CLOSING

Once the home is yours, Murphy Realty / Better Homes and Gardens wants to help you make your moving experience as enjoyable as possible.

Your Murphy Sales Executive can provide you with all types of useful information to ease you into your new community, your new neighborhood and your new home.

Change of address cards, voter registration cards, and a list of telephone numbers to facilitate utility hook ups and telephone installation are just a few of the many helpful items we have available.

13) The next is a Company Credibility Page

Murphy Realty/Better Homes and Gardens
has turned local Real Estate Services into
National Real Estate Systems to help you.

Selling Your Home?   Home Marketing System
Buying a Home?   Home Buying System
Need Information?   Home Information System

Better Homes and Gardens congratulates
Joe Murphy and Allan Dalton for creating
the Home Marketing System.

News Release
2000 Grand Avenue, Des Moines, Iowa 50312

Better Homes and Gardens
Real Estate Service

CONTACT: Gwen Spain
PHONE: 515/284-3131
HOME: 515/232-9475

FOR IMMEDIATE RELEASE

BETTER HOMES AND GARDENS DEVELOPS HOME INFORMATION SYSTEM

Des Moines, Ia.—(June 13, 1985)—Better Homes and Gardens Real Estate Service has announced development of a National Home Information System. This system will allow individuals access to information on housing trends and real estate from Better Homes and Gardens member firms at no obligation. "No longer are we only in the business of helping people buy and sell real estate," said Allen Sabbag, president of the Better Homes and Gardens Real Estate Service. "We are now in the real estate information business."

The Home Information System was initially developed and tested by Murphy Realty/Better Homes and Gardens in New Jersey. According to Murphy Realty executive vice president Allan Dalton, over 5,000 people have requested information through their system since January 1985. Dalton will work with the Real Estate Service to finalize the Home Information System for implementation into Better Homes and Gardens firms across the country. Plans call for the national real estate network to have specifics on financing, economic and housing trends, retirement, relocation and real estate investments. Sabbag said this packaging of housing information is an extension of the commitment to serve consumers with housing needs started by **Better Homes and Gardens** magazine over sixty years ago.

The Real Estate Service is a network of independently owned and operated real estate firms, selected to represent Better Homes and Gardens in their local markets. Established in 1978 by Meredith Corporation, the Fortune 500 company that publishes **Better Homes and Gardens** magazine, the Real Estate Service has grown to approximately 1000 offices in all 50 states.

A WORD OF THANKS
We'd like to thank you for asking Murphy Realty/Better Homes
and Gardens to assist you in the
purchase of your new home.

Now if you have not already created your 'Buying System' or 'Buyer Presentation', you can now use these programs as a catalyst for what you do that is similar, different, and much better... and digital!

Love for you to email me either with what you currently have or, after you create a new system, for feedback and suggestions: allandaltonconsulting@gmail.com

NOTES

_____

_____

_____

_____

_____

_____

_____

_____

_____

SEGMENT 14

WHAT WILL YOU GUARANTEE BUYERS... IF ANYTHING?

This segment will combine **three distinct areas of expressing that you are invaluable to Buyers:**

1) Pledge
2) Guarantee
3) Buyer Presentation

Let's Start with a Pledge

"I have taken Buyer Serve Pledge!" (or words to that effect)

"Ask me about the Buyer Service Pledge!"

A pledge is defined as 'a commitment to a solemn promise'. This suggests that one must be specific in terms of what one is promising yet **not to specific activities.**

Similar to trust, integrity, stability & longevity, one could commit to the following (use your own words):

"I hereby pledge to provide ethical service and sound advice to all Buyers I represent."

Buyers Guarantee

1) "I will listen and learn what my Buyers are seeking in their next home."

2) "I will show all properties, regardless of sources, that I am able to... that are potentially of interest to my Buyers."

3) "I will provide relevant Community information."

4) "I will provide School information."

5) "I will provide complete available property History information."

Buyers Guarantee (cont.)

6) "I will **negotiate in** and **only in the best interests** of my clients when solely representing them."

7) "I will (if asked) arrange for Financing options."

8) "I will professionally manage all of the Transactional Details and keep my Buyer client informed every step of the way."

9) "I will (if needed) help to fairly resolve any Maintenance issues."

10) "I will protect my client's confidentiality."

11) "I will keep in touch with my Buyer clients and help guide them through future maintenance or home improvement needs."

As a Pledge

"Folks, just so you know, I have taken a Buyer-Side Pledge at my Brokerage."

As a Guarantee

"Folks, I would like to review with you my Buyers Guarantee!"

As a Presentation

"Folks, what I do with a lot of my Buyer clients is **I review the steps of a real estate buying process** and **how I serve my Buyers**."

Review List
(with no mention of pledge or guarantee)

"Folks, as you can see the first step in working together is not just to review Buyer Agency and disclosure (which we have just done) but also to share some specifics regarding how I serve and represent the many Buyers whom I am privileged to call clients and then in time friends."

Review List (Cont.)

1) "The first step (for me) is to learn as much as possible regarding your wants, desires, and – as importantly – what you **do not want** in your next home and community. So let's start there."

2) "The second point is that I want you to know I will be representing you and only you (unless the home is one of my own listings), which I will discuss in a moment. This means that all properties – those listed, unlisted, new constriction, and what we refer to as 'for sale by owner' as well as 'withdrawn listings' are up for consideration. As we drive through communities together (or if you do so later on your own) if you see irresistible properties, please let me know! How does that sound to you?"

3) "How important is the neighborhood or community to you? Well, you folks are not alone… as according to the National Association of Realtors®, 75% of Buyers will compromise on the home before they will compromise on the community they prefer!"

(Ed. Note – It is important to have Buyers acknowledge if the community is either very important or the most important when there are things they do not love about the home.)

4) "Because you folks have shared with me the importance of the school system, I will be providing you with very detailed and nuanced information about various schools that would be relevant regarding different communities. Would you also like information on the private schools within the county?"

5) "I will not only be providing you will all available pricing history of Homes you want to drill down on but whenever possible I will put that info in context if I know the market circumstances and the individuals involved. How does that sound?"

6) "Article 1 of the Realtor® Code of Ethics is where Realtors® pledge to 'protect and promote the interests of their clients' and speaks to their Fiduciary Responsibilities. Essentially this means your agent and you should basically 'become as one'. This is my sacred pledge to all of my clients and one of the reasons I love working for the brokerage I do. This means that even if I think you want to buy a certain home, I may discourage you based on a perspective I have that you might not. Is that fair?"

7) "I am also committed to helping you folks establish your purchasing power. This will help us in the negotiating stage."
(Ed. note – notice I didn't mention 'qualifying the Buyer')

8) "Of course, given the ever-growing complexities surrounding home buying, I will stay on top of all of the necessary and administrative details. My partner always complains that I am a stickler for details but I am sure that doesn't bother you."

9) "Because we are in a market that is mature, with many classic homes and developed landscaping, it also means homes have to be maintained. Very frequently, as a condition of a contract, there are maintenance issues and even desired repairs required in order to consummate an agreement between both parties. I will, here again, represent your interests as though I was buying the home myself."

10) "Obviously, anything you share with me that is confidential will remain so. I always include this, folks, in my consultation as I have heard many agents disclose things they should not. For example, "My clients are going through a divorce, so there is pressure to sell"... as opposed to, "My clients are going through a divorce and they have authorized me to reveal this information."

11) "Lastly, just as I have access to a network of home maintenance providers that I have developed over the years, should there be one you need to approve before closing, so too, I make a commitment to all of my Buyer Clients that I will always be there helping them with ongoing home related needs. My clients don't become Past Clients, they become Clients for Life."

Questions

Which of the 11 steps are part of your buying side program?

1. _____   7. _____

2. _____   8. _____

3. _____   9. _____

4. _____   10. _____

5. _____   11. _____

6. _____

Would you be willing to guarantee these steps?

YES   NO

What would you add or take away?

_____

_____

How would you say things differently?

_____

_____

_____

NOTES

SEGMENT 15

ATTRACTING NEW CONSTRUCTION BUYERS

There are a few notable ways to work with Buyers who are interested in new construction.

1) Wait until random Buyers reach out to you or find you through a resale or new construction inquiry.

2) Advertise or create social media-related content to educate Buyers about how to buy new construction.

3) You advertise, "Interested in new construction?" Even If you do not have any new construction listings; and…

4) The most macro of all methods – secure the marketing responsibilities for builders and developers of all sizes.

Since the last option I believe is the most underserved and unseized opportunity for most brokerages, agents, and real estate teams, I am going to focus particularly on how to **secure Buyers by first securing developments.**

BUYER AGENT BE AWARE is comprised of research, best practice interviews with others, and some of my own experiences. Therefore this segment (in order to bring new value) needs to go beyond the mere theoretical.

While very little of this report reflects upon any of my direct brokerage experience, this segment will indeed represent an exception.

I dedicated approximately **twenty years of my brokerage experience**, while president and co-owner of a sixty-office brokerage (built from the ground up), upon securing developments. Securing these developments was immensely gratifying for me both professionally and financially. I was instrumental in bringing into the company, along with my partner (founder and broker of the company), Joe Murphy, dozens of developments. These successes ranged from listing and marketing an entire city called *Newport* – a mixed-use community of retail, commercial, and residential buildings across from Manhattan. *Newport* boasted potentially ten thousand condominiums.

Additionally, we represented numerous luxury home communities, dozens of condominium complexes, and luxury townhouse communities – including Bear's Nest, where President Nixon moved. We marketed President Nixon's estate before he moved to this new community. **I've been told that people like stories so I am adding a little color here.**

My slogan for Bear's Nest was "Why be an empty nester when you can be a Bear's Nester?" I was also the consultant to Atlantic Gulf Developers, who, at that time, was Florida's single largest landowner. Additionally, while president of Move's real estate division, I not only oversaw Realtor.com as its CEO but was responsible for the company's Move Inc. Homebuilder.com website.

I spoke at Home Builder's Association conferences and was invited to be one of two keynote speakers at London's Dorchester Hotel during the **UK's Builders Association black tie event**. The keynote speaker the year before (politics aside) was Donald Trump. From that background, the following will be my recommendations for increasing Buyer-side share in the new construction and the New Dev realm.

Case study: Newport

The Lefrak organization (Google them) built numerous apartment buildings throughout New York City, Long Island, and Queens. They had never before hired a real estate brokerage to represent any of their developments during the pre-construction stage or during the selling phases, which represented the initial sale of their properties to Buyers. LeFrak decided that because this was their first foray across the Hudson River, they would interview both marketing agencies in New York as well as multiple large brokerages and brands in New Jersey. I appreciate that no one reading this is as interested in what happened then as they are in discerning how what I am sharing relates to their present and future ability to secure new construction projects and major developments.

To the developers, we presented:

1) "**You don't need us to sell your several thousand condominiums** because you can sell them yourselves. You need us, however, if you want to market them. You might sell out these buildings, yet that is the last thing you want to do. Instead, you want to **maximize the marketing so you can sell your condominiums at the highest possible prices.** All pricing is governed by the laws of supply and demand and, therefore, the more we increase the demand through our range, reach, and influence, the higher your prices can be!"

Networking:

2) "Yes, as you are a major developer, **you can also do some advertising** but you cannot effectively network. We have twelve hundred 'hungry mouths to feed' and there are twenty thousand other agents with whom we can network who would love to be able to tell everyone in their geographic farms and client bases, that 'there is now an opportunity to live in the glow of the Manhattan skyline yet not pay Manhattan prices!"

3) "Another reason we will be able to mobilize our entire organization is that we need to **provide our agents with a greater reason to contact homeowners** and this way they can also secure their listings!"

4) "We will also offer a **lower marketing fee** to anyone who sells their home and buys at Newport."

5) "Because we have sixty offices in Northern New Jersey, two in Manhattan, and three right here in Jersey City, we will create a *Newport City Counseling Information Center* and **provide Newport materials at each strategically located venue.**"

6) "Because this area is so diversified, we will feature Newport on the cover of **four-color homes guides in the following six languages**: Russian, Spanish, Chinese, Korean, Japanese, and English (and featured in magazines in those languages) to attract and appeal to the broadest range of Buyers by also **making each segment more at home.**"

7) "I already had our **"director of feng shui"** review the site and floor plans and he resoundingly approved. While I cannot speak Chinese, he physically gave me two thumbs up."

8) Here are the telemarketing scripts we have prepared for our telemarketing division.

9) We would like to offer a **Rent to Buy Assistance Program** to these seven high-rise rental buildings along the river and let prospective renters or Buyers know that they have been approved for up to three months of their lease payments, assumed by you the developer, or a point taken off their mortgage if they "move up" to Newport.

10) We will present to you **an award from our brand** for your transforming this space (which we did).

11) Here is an example of the sales scripts for the agents we select to work onsite.

12) Notice how we handle every objection within our Newport professional sales consultation scripts.

13) Because most people visit and then start making decisions after they leave, we hired Del Wade of Channel 4 NY to tape this message about Newport.

14) We can also have a vertical pricing team help with the pricing for every unit, every line, based upon sq footage, views, floor level, distance to the elevator, etc., and we will coach our agents on selling upgrades with special training as a requirement for working onsite.

15) Here are the three campaigns we recommend:

The first would feature how Newport is at the end of the Lincoln Tunnel, "Newport the light at the end of the tunnel."

Because the train from Manhattan to New Jersey is called the PATH, I have created: "Newport… Your path to a better lifestyle".

For those taking the ferry back and forth across the river: "Don't miss the boat. Move over Manhattan".

16) Because we called our marketing division "Metro Media", here are the ads and press releases we would look to do.

17) Because Buyers are also considering many options, all of our licensed salespeople would be able to keep Buyers here and not roam because they have tremendous knowledge of all Gold Coast inventory as opposed to your hiring regular salespeople who do not know the entire market.

18) Anyone who does not buy here that we refer, you would receive a referral fee … but we want you to send shoppers in as we guarantee we will only look to sell Newport.

19) We can provide financing through our New Jersey-based lenders.

20) Now we would like to share with you our reporting system (which was world-class).

21) Here is how we will stay in touch and keep reinforcing all of the non-binding reservations Buyers, along with the newsletter we would call "Newport Matters."

22) We would like to have within our marketing pieces a "Developers Legacy" about your storied history in development.

23) We did a S.W.O.T. analysis on your development and would like to share it with you.

24) At our annual awards, we honor those who excel in new development selling. Would you present some awards with us?

For each development, we had a complete solution – including event marketing, interior design, and public relations. There are too many to review here. Instead, let's examine **what might work for you today.**

DISCUSSION POINTS

For all those who are either brokers, marketing managers, office managers, trainers, coaches, team leaders, or big-thinking real estate professionals.

1. Do you like the distinction regarding selling versus marketing?

                         YES   NO

2. Marketing versus networking?   YES   NO

3. How would you add social media and AI to your presentation?

_____

4. What about showing designed telemarketing and on-site sales scripts?

_____

5. With so many luxury condo and mixed communities being luxury branded as Ritz Carlton, Four Seasons or Fairmont, do you think it would help to make the point that your brand – which would be involved in the marketing and sales – could also make a major difference?
Do you agree?

                                                                        YES   NO

6. Would it help to have a press release prepared?   YES   NO

7. How about having marketing campaigns already prepared as part of your presentation?   YES   NO

8. How about targeting other buildings or feeder markets through Chalk Digital as part of your presentation?   YES   NO

9. How do you show your reports that track traffic and help you adjust marketing and maybe pricing?

---

10. Do you like the idea of saying, "You don't need me to sell but you do to market and network"?   YES   NO

11. Did you like how I addressed diversity and feng shui?   YES   NO

Do you think these issues are relevant today?   YES   NO

12. What did you think about explaining that you would have your telemarketers use the scripts and conduct research on behalf of the development through conducting approved surveys?   YES   NO

DISCUSSION POINTS (Cont.)

13. How does your present approach to securing
developments compare to these points?   Y E S   N O

14. How can you use all of your brokerage or where applicable brand or
network resources?

_____

_____

_____

Would builders be impressed with any content you have
regarding children if the development includes families?   Y E S   N O

Would they be impressed with any content you have
regarding pets should the housing community allow pets?   Y E S   N O

Would that make sense to include downsizing content in
certain development presentations?   Y E S   N O

Info about renting versus buying in certain communities?   Y E S   N O

Will you tell a developer that you will put together a guide
of local services for their new residents with a cover letter
from the developer?   Y E S   N O

Should you explain your use of video, social media, and
your CRM?   Y E S   N O

Additional recommendations and discussions:

Consider taking a course on new construction.

Consider joining a Home Builder's Association and attend events.

Consider conducting new construction seminars and invite the builders you wish to represent.

Additional Thoughts:

This is what typically happens after all phases of a new development are sold out: Two or three agents who live there will say they are "a Pleasant Hill Townhomes specialist." That is a micro idea. **Here is a macro one** that worked for me and my company:

Announce the "Pleasant Hill Customized Resale Marketing System" available to all homeowners of Pleasant Hill.

Reason: Before the development was sold out, it enjoyed wholesale marketing, videos, community brochures, etc. After it sells out, it moves to retail marketing only (i.e. the marketing of unit 302 versus the macro-marketing of the entire development for all the current residents).

Here is how you can "bring back wholesale marketing" to a development that has been sold out:

1) Create a "Customized Pleasant Hill Resale Marketing System."

2) You can also do a video of the whole development, now that people live there. You will get listings by asking them for testimonials and potential Buyers by distributing your current community video.

3) You might want to replicate this idea: I took out a full page in a major newspaper with this message, "Thanks to New Jersey builders for all they do as, without them, we would not have our jobs ... and you would not have your homes."

I said this as this is exactly what I believe and feel!

Summary

For those familiar with my industry contributions and systems throughout the years, you may recall how passionately, and presumably logically, I spoke to the need to evolve from **listing presentations to marketing proposals** when one is seeking to secure residential listings.

I personalized this segment more than all others in an attempt to also influence the manner in which many brokerages I know, team leaders, and top individual real estate agents approach builders. From all of my experience and research, I am convinced that many builders and **developers are still approached** through a "listing presentation paradigm" vs a "customized marketing proposal."

Please note that in my outline of my approach, there was no mention of **how great our company was** or information about us as leaders.

lease note that in my outline of my approach, there was no mention of **how great our company was** or information about us as leaders.

Now, obviously, you will include a more digital emphasis on social media, market data, artificial intelligence, and video as these are the new variables but the fundamentals must never be ignored and always be showcased. **"It's about the community and the developer and not us."**

I hope this helps and that you will use this workbook to discuss these wildly successful methods at your office, company, team, or in your training level. I hope that these discussions (unless you are already having them to this level of detail) will result in a resolution to do more business than ever with new construction builders ... and "Buyers."

Lastly, the reason why I focused more on how to attract new construction Buyers by first securing that inventory is also due to the following likelihood: Specifically, the more that Buyers believe that they are expected to pay a fee to a Buyer's Agent, the more they will most likely be inclined to **go directly to the builder or developer** ... which means that real estate brokerages and agents must become more instrumental in the **sales and marketing of new construction.**

NOTES

SEGMENT 16

CREATING BUYER EVENTS

Most real estate professionals focus more on the micro aspects of the real estate business than they do on the macro. This is because real estate, for most, began with the following pronouncement:
"I am going to become a real estate salesperson!"

Far fewer new-to-the-business real estate professionals proclaimed:
"I am going to be a **real estate marketing person**!"

To some, this may represent a **distinction without a difference** while others will immediately recognize the importance of words and even recall the following anonymous quote:

"Watch your thoughts because your thoughts become your words, your words become your actions, your actions become your behavior, your behavior becomes your character and your character becomes your destiny!"

To that point, the fact that real estate licenses read "real estate salesperson" and not "real estate marketing person" ... or that the industry, writ large, still fancies the term "listing agent" over "marketing agent" and "listing presentations" over "marketing proposals" clearly supports the consequences of those thoughts and words.

"Real estate salespeople" **are transactional** and therefore focus mostly on the parties to a transaction.

As an example a sales person by definition focuses more on the parties to a transaction... as in wondering if a Buyer or seller is more verbal then visual, or a D-type personality or a C, and therefore acting somewhat as a sales consultant and employing the psychology of sales.

This is what "salespeople" do to deal with the issues of individuals or **micro and not macro groups**. "Micro real estate" is everything a salesperson does **at the bottom of the sales funnel.**

A great way to create a high impact at the macro level is through event marketing, and, specifically, through **educational events and public seminars** ... either physically or virtually

Ironically, while real estate professionals are certainly no strangers to seminars the following may very well be true:

"Real estate professionals perhaps, more than any other professional, attend the most seminars ... **while themselves conducting the fewest!**"

Here is a guide to conducting public seminars for Buyers.

Step 1 – Your "Why"

A. To educate the public (including Clients, prospects, friends, family, and followers) regarding real estate opportunities and overall market conditions and trends.

B. To build relationships, gain trust, and create Clients.

C. Leverage your brand and the respect of your local brokerage.

Step 2 – Decide on the Name of the Event

A. Home Buyer's Expo

B. Home Buyer's Night

C. Home Buyer's Symposium

D. Home Buyer's Public Open House Seminar

E. First Time Buyer's (etc.)

An alternative:

For years I conducted "Real Estate Town Meetings."

Hundreds came out to each event and the printed agenda was:

- Learn about Community Real Estate Values
- How to Appeal Your Property Taxes
- Learn New Developments
- Strategies for First-Time, Move-Up, and Downsizing Buyers and Sellers
- How to Make Your Home More Valuable
- Refinancing Your Home

Step 3 – Chose Sponsors & Presentation Partners

A. Chose presenters who are not boring but entertainingly informative

B. Chose partners who have sales teams to help promote the event

C. Chose partners who will provide a gift that you can promote

Step 4 – Select Location (if physical)

A. Hotels

B. Banquet halls

C. Realtor and MLS venues

D. Schools

E. Libraries

F. Other

Step 5 – Select a Time

Tuesday, Wednesday and Thursday evenings are most suitable.

Step 6 – Develop Your Presentations (power point and beyond)

1. Welcome audience (start on time)

2. Introduce yourself and speaking partners and sponsors

3. Offer the purpose of the event

4. Outline the agenda and promise when it will end

5. Include enough time for question and answer period

6. Prepare a Call to Action

Step 7 – Call to Action

Ask for emails from all those who:

a. Want copies of the PowerPoint

b. Want links to materials

c. Want to receive Zoom invitations

d. Want market updates

e. Have everyone fill out a survey & provide testimonials for the program

Materials to bring, subjects to cover and more...

- How to appeal property taxes (print out instructions from Google)

- Brochures about moving with children and/or pets

- Brochures regarding downsizing or "moving up"

- Information about how to buy or sell when divorcing

- Bring a "How can I help you this year?" survey

- Information about how to appeal property taxes

- Show a video encouraging homeownership!

- How to promote and market through CRM, Database, Client Base and Social Media and do a video overview invitation.

- Include QR code registration

- Follow up one and two nights before with all registrants and invitees

- Have flyers at all open houses

- Ask local restaurants and businesses to showcase invitation

- Contact local TV and radio stations to announce

- Ask clergypeople to announce at their services

- Contact each attendee with a thank you note and phone call after

- Virtual events

Since we are several years past COVID, which triggered a world of virtual seminars and events, we all know the convenience and power of virtual meetings. A major difference between "a Zoom meeting" and a "Buyer's Zoom meeting" is that the latter **must be technologically perfect.** Not that "perfection" shouldn't be the goal at physically attended events as well but there is more forgiveness when technology goes wrong when it is merely a part of an event ... versus the overwhelmingly predicate for the event.

At a hotel or library, attendees are looking at many features throughout the event: the decor, the other attendees, walls, ceilings, and additional speakers... **virtually the screen is the whole show!** There is never any forgiveness online and they don't get to meet other people and have free refreshments! Therefore your presentation, voice modulation, whether you use a gallery to reveal attendees, whether you record and announce you are recording, etc. must all be prepared and perfect. Accordingly, **several trial runs to simulate the event are a must!**

Your visuals (videos and all graphics) must be forensically addressed before the event and you should never reveal the number of attendees ... unless it is overwhelmingly impressive! More than anything else (as is the case with a physical event) you are "auditioning." The success of the event will foretell how you will be successful in representing Clients!

If you do not have a successful event (either through a lack of attendance or a lackluster performance) **you will pay a price.** The only benefit to you of a small turnout is that only a few people will be aware the event was lackluster. **You need to promote attendance** (either for an online or offline event) with the **same level of zeal as a passionate protestor encouraging attendance at a rally** ... and you need to do a press release before, after, and then **showcase the video of the event** afterward on social media channels or stream in real-time.

PROPSED FLYER DESIGN

As I live in a world of reality and not theory, I seek to show examples of how I implemented that which I am espousing whenever possible. Although I can only show the past (versus what I might do in the future), the finishing flyer is what I did then and is the ultimate 'Macro Concept'. While some of my competitors were doing Buyers' or First-Time Buyers' Nights at hotels, I was painting on a much larger and more macro canvas… and holding 'Real Estate Town Meeting' events at local town halls and country clubs.

This is what 'representing a community means'… while everyone else was mimicking one another with how they, "Served the community!"

NOTES

SEGMENT 17

BUYERS NEED & LOVE COMMUNITY VIDEOS

I believe one of the most strategic and successful methods of attracting both Buyers and Sellers is through the production of **world-class, long-form community videos** that are not intended for indiscriminate and random social media and internet visitors but rather to be directed specifically to **interested Buyers and Home Sellers through email**, Chalk Digital promotion, CRMs, and usage at Open Houses. To fully grasp the very material benefits of creating riveting community lifestyle stories requires first considering other **options of scaling attention, interest, and engagement with Buyers and Sellers**.

Thus, please consider these questions:

What percentage of people who someday might either buy or sell a home in your market would you guess **know of you**? _____ %

What percentage of these folks **when they think of buying or selling a home in your market think of you**? _____ %

If you surveyed every potential Buyer or Seller in your market and asked, "Which real estate agent possesses the greatest knowledge about the community and its overall lifestyle and does the best job of promoting your town."
How many would you guess would name you first? _____ %

After reflecting upon those questions, consider the following:

How much more would you like to be known, respected, and valued in each of those three situations? _____ %

If your answer is, "It doesn't matter much," and, "I never think about questions like this," then the following information **will be of no interest or use to you.** On the contrary, if you believe it is important that when Buyers and Sellers think of real estate or think of **who knows the most about the community** that they think of you, then I respectfully invite you to continue reading and "thinking."

The number one method, in the opinion of this real estate consultant, to improve your statistics in each of these scenarios is through producing world-class, riveting, unforgettable, comprehensive, highly relevant, and accurate community video narratives.

Why are world-class community videos, which reflect your passion, professionalism, and knowledge regarding the lifestyles of the communities where you market homes for Sellers and educate Buyers **so extraordinarily timely and important?**

For five reasons:

1) If you want to become the real estate talk of the town, you need to be known as the most knowledgeable person who talks about the town!

2) The marketing of "homes" has become somewhat, if not mostly, commoditized and offers fewer opportunities to differentiate value than the marketing of communities. Every agent presumably markets homes, while less than 5% (if that) have ever produced a world-class long-form community video.

3) 75 % of Buyers are willing to compromise more on the home they purchase than the community they select.

4) Community storytelling can be used as a prospecting tool to gather community testimonials and comments.

5) Community marketing appeals to Buyers, Sellers, Homeowners, and local businesses.

Plus, Community Videos represent the ultimate in macro versus micro marketing!

This is because the word "Community" is defined as: "A group of people living in the same place or having a particular characteristic in common."

I invite you to reflect upon that definition. Ask yourself, "What does that definition mean to me?"

To me, it means that since the only way one has access to others is through their concerns, then the most macro real estate idea, and potentially the most lucrative, must be through **community marketing** – because everyone who owns a home or might buy a home has a shared interest in the perceived value of real estate within that community.

Let's examine why this is so:

If you want to create the optimum visibility campaign within your markets or communities how would you go about it considering that the only way to have access is through people's concerns?

How about becoming more active within your house of worship? Well, if there are fifty thousand people in town, that might include one thousand who could get to know you and come to respect you. Plus, there are many fellow real estate worshipers competing.

Also, within that group, there might exist different political views and a wide range of other disqualifying (for you) attributes as fellow worshippers get to know more about your political views.

Same with all other smaller groups or micro markets.

Yet those communities within communities are also bound together in the same way as the larger community coalesces. Specifically, the largest community unites around the shared values and interests of all people who live in the community ... their home values! That is **the number one club** you want to belong to and the only way you can not only join it but lead it is to do something no other member of the town can do: dramatically promote its overall home values!

1) All homeowners want their home values to appreciate. A community video impacts the perception of the community and therefore appeals to its value.

2) All renters and prospective Buyers either want to feel pride in where they live or want validation for buying in the town ... which the video validates.

3) All Home Sellers want Buyers to fully grasp the whole story of the town ... which only a long-form (7-12 min) video can accomplish!

How should a community video be prepared, and produced and what is the desired length?

The answer to length depends upon usage.

For social media, a community video (based on Google and YouTube metrics) should not be longer than one or two minutes. This is long enough to give Buyers a "feel of a community" and a great way to promote you, the agent.

Yet this somewhat superficial level of stitched-together snippets does not even remotely grasp the significance of the town's schools, recreation, history, restaurants, commuting times, and individual neighborhoods. Therefore it is underwhelming in regard to somebody deciding which agent they want to either market their home or educate them on the community.

The greatest byproduct of doing a 2-minute snippet on social media is the expected complaints from anybody who lives there regarding everything **that was left out** or that it was too much about the non-charismatic agent (speaking of non-charismatic, that would be me!) Unfortunately Hollywood is too busy making movies to attend real estate conventions to do screen tests.

To accomplish high-level engagement amongst community homeowners, here is what I did as the founder of TownAdvisor. As one who has authored and produced dozens of videos, let me assure you that **no ninety-second or two-minute video will ever cause homeowners to proudly send a link to friends and relatives as a way of boasting about their town.**

A **home can be captured in two or three minutes and a condo building or golf course** yet not so when it comes to complex and comprehensive community storytelling that satisfies the education interest of Buyers contemplating where they might live for the next ten years.

This factor calls into play this next question:
"Will anyone watch a video for 7 to 10 minutes?"

Absolutely! Yet only the people you wish to influence who are legitimate Buyers, pridefully Sellers who recognize that the town story is part of their home-for-sale story, as well as local merchants, and relocation directors.

Here are some of the reasons why there is a difference between capturing somebody with interest over seeking "passerby clicks" with a high dropoff rate. If you tell people that you're going to post educational online videos and ask them how long they should be, how many do you believe would say, "about twenty minutes," versus, "two, five, or six?"

Well, thankfully TED Talks didn't succumb to "such wisdom" as their average video is almost 20 mins!

How many of you would pay thirty or forty thousand dollars for a ninety-second or two-minute video of a wedding?

Of course, you would not, and here's why: Because you have a high level of interest! On the contrary, I won't take more than sixty seconds on an educational video if I'm not interested … or it's not extremely well done … but I will on some of the subjects TED Talks cover.

I won't watch a celebrity wedding video but I have watched my daughters' 2-hour wedding video time and time again (especially my 2 minutes in the video).

I will not spend more than <u>ninety seconds</u> watching a community video if I am not considering moving to that community or if it's not where I live … **especially if it is more about the agent than the town**! Yet, as I mentioned, I will take ten minutes to learn more about where I might live for the next dozen or more years. **Wouldn't you?**

<u>Here is an example of a long-form lifestyle narrative of Charlotte</u> which I wrote and Ryan Ward produced and narrated for **Kathleen Rebhan**. You can prompt Chat GPT and other language models one hundred different ways and they will not match or exceed this storytelling!!!

The key is that ten-minute videos are <u>not for posting online</u> they are for:

- Emailing to homeowners

- Emailing to prospective Buyers

- Showing on open house loops to secure email addresses

- Social media platforms and programs (like Chalk Digital)

- Sending through your CRM to every single homeowner that you have an email for in all of your local markets

Again the audience is not the 8 billion humans on the planet yet it is for the **five to ten thousand homeowners** and all of the Buyers considering that community.

People can not find what they are not searching for and most will not know that you have done a video. Yet, if you are linking your website to all of your social media and on your website you have **different towns with long-form videos** the right people will receive this powerful message regarding your being an advocate or advisor for all the communities in your market Also, a community video is a great pre-listing/marketing tool and for marketing proposals.

Seller: "Mr. Dalton, who will get to see this amazing video?"

Dalton: "Folks, feel free to call me Allan, but to answer your question every single Buyer who comes to me or through the open houses will see the video. The video is not to attract Buyers to the town; that's not necessary. Because all marketing comes down to three words: range, reach, and influence, we use the video to influence Buyers after our range and reach brings them to the home."

With Out-of-Town Buyers:

"Folks, you are asking about the schools. I produced a video on the town that covers schools and a lot more. Would you like me to send to you?"

"You asked about the transportation and commuting times. Would you like me to send you a video that covers that?"

"You asked about the beaches may I send you a video that covers that?"

Next consideration: In producing a video, what do you believe is more important: The images OR the narration?

I asked this question to **dozens of audiences** and the overwhelming consensus was that "the visuals" were more important. Then we did the following test:

1) I would show the video with visuals and music but no text, and then...

2) Show the video but only play narration and music with no visuals...

Then I would ask the audience:

"Which impressed you the most?"

"Which was more informative?"

"Which could influence your decision on where to move and buy?"

Without exception, the responses were always, "the narration," but more importantly and overwhelmingly everyone also said, "You need both!"

Clearly, you need both. A movie with just dialogue or a picture without words is seldom successful (although one with no dialogue won an Oscar but remember the captioning was still on the screen).

This is because ocean waves, pictures of mountains, downtown areas, train stations, and Starbucks are somewhat baked into what people already know about the areas they are considering.

How much would you be surprised to see a beach in a Florida town versus how surprised you might be to learn that the town was third safest in the state, the commute into the city was only thirty minutes, the educational scores were exceptional, and there were five hundred acres of dedicated parks!

Information is what they don't have. Images are already in their heads!

1) Don't just focus on the positives but also deal with any major negatives. Treat the town story as if you were defending it in court. While everything must be true you are advocating for the town on behalf of the community (because at that time you are not representing anybody as a client) while also being transparent and accurate for Buyers.

Let me provide some examples of text:

a) **In towns where the school system is seen by some as a negative, you can state:** "Many homeowners take advantage of the lower prices and taxes by utilizing those savings to send their children to some of the most prestigious private schools in the country. Therefore, living closer to the city, they can buy more home for their money and provide a superior education for the children. This lifestyle is also coveted by the many affluent families who also place a premium on diversity and a pedestrian-friendly urban downtown."

Let me provide some examples of text:

Watch the Video Here

b) **If a town is considered too remote, state**: "The town of Weston, CT, perhaps as much as any elite community within Metropolitan New York, has painstakingly preserved its relative anonymity, remarkable tranquility, and solitude that its 20.7 square miles of sacred parks, forests, farms, and waterways (located approximately fifty miles from New York City) provides its deeply satisfied residents. The town's penchant for privacy aside, it is an ideal choice not only for those seeking family living at its fullest but also for those who crave a level of natural beauty and peaceful living that serves as a stark contrast to the intense demands their high profile careers."

c) **When a city is considered looking to re-invent itself because of its past reputation:** "Decades ago Buffalo Springfield iconically wrote and sang, 'There's something happening here. What it is ain't exactly clear...' Many years later there is something happening in Bridgeport ... but what's happening, in this case, is very clear! Whether what is taking place is defined as a Renaissance, Rebirth, or Revitalization, it is abundantly obvious that Connecticut's most populous city (located 60 miles from New York City) is currently being transformed into a most compelling place to either live, locate a business to, visit, or invest!"

Divide the video's segments into either Top 5 or Top 10 reasons to live in the town or city and make sure (like any good book or narrative film) your video has a theme.

<u>Here are examples of mine</u>:
1) A move to New Jersey is "**A Genius Decision!**"

Watch the Video Here

Because geniuses Albert Einstein and Thomas Edison both voluntarily moved to New Jersey, I picked that as my theme. Also, because Edison invented the light bulb, I wrote, "In order to make the genius decision to move to New Jersey a light bulb [which is shown] must first go of ... and by the way, the light bulb itself was made in New Jersey!"

2) Norwalk, CT used to be known as "Oyster Town," therefore the opening for that town's video was, "Welcome to Norwalk, where the world is your oyster!"

3) As Fairfield, CT has two universities, my opening was, "Fairfield, your educated choice!"

Indeed community videos can help you show greater Buyer-side Value while also helping you represent more Sellers.

In preparation for your town or city video, list the ten greatest reasons to buy in your town/city or a town/city you market:

1 _____   6 _____

2 _____   7 _____

3 _____   8 _____

4 _____   9 _____

5 _____   10 _____

———————•❧•———————

FINAL NOTE:
Should you have an interest in Ryan and me producing an impactful, community video for your town, towns or city... contact us at either:

allandaltonconsulting@gmail.com or ryanthedesigner@gmail.com

NOTES

SEGMENT 18

SOCIAL MEDIA MARKETING CONTENT AND BUYERS

This particular segment focuses on the inevitable integration of social media marketing and purposefully prepared professional pertinent and proactive content. The specific emphasis of this content will be directed, as is the case of all segments, for the relationship between social media marketing content and the pursuit and cultivation of Buyer Clients.

The reason why the subjects of social media and content, while different in name, are being treated as one is that together they are as inseparable as the terms "the internet" and "the web". The internet and the web, while each being codependent, also possess distinct properties. This same combination of separation and synergy also is the case in how social media platforms and content can be viewed either as stand-alone or as symbiotically working together.

Another example of how iconic developments seamlessly work together is again the relationship between the internet and the web. While the Internet preceded the World Wide Web by twenty or so years, it is common for many to use these terms interchangeably. "I am going to search the web" or "I am going to search the internet" are both acceptable references.

The reason why our age has been called the Information Age is because of both the internet and the web.

- Web 1.0 represented the presentation of websites and non-interactive information.

- Web 2.0 spawned terms like citizen journalism and the democratization of information.

Citizen journalism clearly does and should include the involvement of real estate professionals yet to become a social media content provider or citizen journalist requires content ... both visual and textual.

The real estate industry thankfully, and understandably, did not have to create any of today's important real estate-related technologies. Consumers use Google, but no real estate brand or brokerage introduced this informational juggernaut. So too Facebook, YouTube, Instagram, LinkedIn, etc., did not organically emerge within real estate industry think tanks.

Regrettably, for many in the real estate industry there existed early on the confusion surrounding social media optimization. This missed opportunity, due to a lack of clarity, was a direct result of a lack of distinctiveness surrounding the differences between social networking, social media, and social media marketing. This confusion or conflation impeded the appropriate use of social media platforms for scores of bewildered real estate professionals. That said, while tens of thousands of real estate professionals wallowed in mediocrity the more technological and marketing savvy agents flourished. In order to maximize social media platforms requires a basic understanding of the purpose and premise behind different types of activity.

1) Social networking means using the above-mentioned platforms to make and keep friends.

2) Social media means to bring content to these platforms.

3) Social media marketing means creating content that pertains to the needs of the real estate marketplace. Please match the following three forms of content with their appropriate definition ... are these activities social networking, social media, or social media marketing?

a. Posting a video of your trip to Niagara Falls?

    social networking • social media • social media marketing

b. Posting information of a historical speech or quote?

    social networking • social media • social media marketing

c. Posting information on how to become a first-time home Buyer?

    social networking • social media • social media marketing

Fortunately, it is now possible through Artificial Intelligence and predictive data to determine which keywords, hashtags, communities, and demographics are best engaged in our attention society. Moreover, it is also now knowable to learn through a simple Google search which content enjoys the most clicks and ROI on various platforms and how to shape videos and text based on different distribution channels.

There is also a need for you to do research that only applies to your situation as follows:

What percentage of your friends, fans, and followers on Facebook, LinkedIn, Instagram, TikTok, YouTube, etc.

- Are fellow real estate agents? _____%

- Are homesellers who live in your market?

- Are they potential Buyers?

- How many household owners who live in your market are connected to you consistently on social media platforms?

How much of your social media content is specifically directed to particular communities, networks, neighborhoods, or civic groups?

Since video constitutes around 80 percent of what consumers click on, how would you rate from 1 to 5, the following:

- Your video content 1 to 5

- Video distribution 1 to 5

How often do you use YouTube? Never, seldom, frequently:

- For tutorials
- For educational reasons
- For comedy
- To entertain
- To showcase property
- To showcase community
- To appeal to Buyers
- To appeal to homesellers
- Other

How do you use TikTok?

- For tutorials
- For educational reasons
- For comedy
- To entertain
- To showcase property
- To showcase community
- To appeal to Buyers
- To appeal to homesellers

Facebook

- For tutorials
- For educational reasons
- For comedy
- To entertain
- To showcase property
- To showcase community
- To appeal to Buyers
- To appeal to homesellers

Instagram
- For tutorials
- For educational reasons
- For comedy
- To entertain
- To showcase property
- To showcase community
- To appeal to Buyers
- To appeal to homesellers

Other
- For tutorials
- For educational reasons
- For comedy
- To entertain
- To showcase property
- To showcase community
- To appeal to Buyers
- To appeal to homesellers

LinkedIn
- To post resume
- To network
- To provide thought leadership
- To promote property

The importance of creating effective content!

Having distribution **without great content** is ineffective.

Having **great content** without distribution is also ineffective.

Thankfully there are plenty of free distribution channels. All of the social media platforms listed on the previous page can be used as distribution channels by customizing your content and uploading it on all of these platforms.

Content Creation
I suggest your content conforms to my five Ps.

1) Purposeful

2) Prepared

3) Professional

4) Pertinent

5) Proactive

Purposeful

What is your why or purpose for creating and distributing content?
Rate 1 to 5 (with 5 being your greatest motivation or intent) for each:

- To educate Buyers and Sellers   1   2   3   4   5

- To build my personal brand   1   2   3   4   5

- My desire to write text   1   2   3   4   5

- My desire to creatively produce videos   1   2   3   4   5

- To create exposure for my properties   1   2   3   4   5

- To market my communities   1   2   3   4   5

- To generate referrals   1   2   3   4   5

Prepared

- How much research do you do in creating content?

    A LITTLE • MODERATE • A LOT

- Do you rely on sources like Inman, Ris Media, etc.?

    YES   NO

- Do you rely on content/programs developed by the brokerage?

    YES   NO

- Do you rely on content and marketing created by your brand?

    YES   NO

- Do you post most or all of your social media content yourself or have a social media distribution manager like Real Grader?

    MYSELF   MANAGER

Professional

How would you rate the professional level of the following activities?

- Your business profile   1 2 3 4 5

- Your picture   1 2 3 4 5

- Your text   1 2 3 4 5

- Your video quality   1 2 3 4 5

- The relevance of your content   1 2 3 4 5

- Your distribution   1 2 3 4 5

Real Grader can help you grade and assess your effectiveness in each of these activities plus enhance your results on any and all of these social media platforms.

Pertinent

How pertinent is your content to the needs of Buyers, sellers, and the community at large?

1   2   3   4   5

List the pertinent content that you have created for Buyers beyond property information.

_____	_____
_____	_____
_____	_____

What percentage of your content is video?   _____ %

Proactive

- How much attention do you pay to SEO?

    None   Very little   Some   A lot

- How much do you spend on social boosting?

    None   Very little   Some   A lot

- Do you use Chalk Digital to proactively geo-target markets?

    None   Very little   Some   A lot

- Do you use predictive data to proactively distribute to target markets?

    None   Very little   Some   A lot

Summary

In the information age, the number of educational resources, best practices, coaching, and overall strategies surrounding both social media, its content, and its integration is immense, ever-growing, and ever-changing. That said, this segment does not presume to tell you what you may already know or can readily research on your own. Rather, its purpose is to challenge your fundamental views regarding how you THINK!

Specifically, to make sure that you do not replicate what has been a decades-long obsession with personal promotion offline and merely look to transport that tendency online.

NOTES

_____

_____

_____

_____

_____

_____

SEGMENT 19

ATTRACTING AND ENGAGING OUT-OF-TOWN BUYERS

Let's do the math!

1) According to the NAR 2023 Home Buyer's Research, when Buyers are considering where to move they look at properties, on average, which are located within a 26-mile radius. This area of exploration is down from a 50-mile radius during COVID but more expansive than the 15 miles where properties were in consideration before COVID.

2) The number one Buyer's consideration (60%) for home selection was a specific town or neighborhood over the home itself.

3) 32 % of Buyers were first-time Buyers

4) 34 % moved because of a job

5) 34 % moved to be closer to a relative

6) The three next "largest pools" of Buyers are folks retiring, looking for a lifestyle change, and seeking home affordability

7) This statistic is from the author of this buyer side resource, "While at Realtor.com our metrics indicated that over 98% of visitors to the site (all of whom had an equal opportunity to click on either "Find a Home' or "Find an Agent") clicked "Find a Home."

8) 70 % of Buyers only end up using one Agent

9) The average Buyer looks at an average of ten homes offline

10) 90 % of Buyers indicate they intend to use their Agent again

You are invited to ask yourself, "What does this all mean," or, "What should I do regarding each of these statistics?" The following are some suggested ways to think about these statistical factors:

1) Because of the combined range and reach of the internet/web, more than ever, real estate Agents can exponentially reach and influence Buyers earlier on in the buying search process ... but this **requires an 'Out-of-Area Buyer plan'.**

2) **Because 75 % of Buyers will compromise on the home** and 60 % list "community information" as most important, this challenges you to **include community profiles** in your overall Buyer-side business plan, personal website, videos online, and on social media ... information for out-of-area Buyers of communities.

3) Because of the high percentage of first-time Buyers, it is recommended that you develop a **"Guide for First-Time Buyers"** which you can post or link; even if they are out of town.

4) **34 % of Buyers move because of a job.** Consider creating a "welcome wagon"-like gift package from local merchants and promote it online ("Ask about my welcome-to-town gift package!") and let Relo departments and home services divisions know that you can make this available through them.

5) **34 % of out-of-area Buyers move to be closer to relatives.** As simple as it is, consider messaging such as, "If you are looking to move closer to your family, call me today!" You can then use Chalk Digital or knock on doors on behalf of their families to increase options right on their street or neighborhood to be even closer to their relatives.

6) **Regarding people retiring** – create:

- a 'senior lifestyle division'
- a 'senior lifestyle brochure'
- videos with "the top-ten questions every senior should ask about real estate"
- advertise: "When seniors are making lifestyle changes, they start with (name)!"

The more people in the community who associate you as the pronounced go-to person for seniors, the more they will reach out to you on behalf of their loved ones.

7) While 98 % of visitors clicked on "Find a Home" versus "Find an Agent," over 84 % ended up with an Agent! **This means that they will end up with you either through:**

- Paid results
- Compelling contents
- Social boosting
- World-class open houses
- The best virtual tours
- Best videos
- Referrals

8) **70 % only use one agent.** This should increase, as Buyer-side contracts and Buyer-side fees expectedly increase. Thus, if between 70 and 100 % of Buyers only work with one agent moving forward, this is all the more incentive to leverage how you can strategically engage out-of-area Buyers as the ROI is more assured.

9) **Buyers only look at ten homes offline on average.** If 70 % or more people stay with their Buyer Agent and then only look, on average, at ten homes … this means two things:

a. Much of their search is done without you which saves you time and you are not paying for this effort

b. It is all the more reason that you invest in your image, profile, virtual tours, and in all other ways you can engage, impress, and influence Buyers before their physical search … and all the greater incentive to communicate compelling knowledge while revealing your skills in the following ways:

- Your knowledge of the community
- Your negotiating skills
- Your trustworthiness
- The look and feel of all of your marketing
- Your strategic placement of testimonials and reviews
- Your use of content

Content for Out-of-Area Buyers

- Content when moving with children (with video and textual content links)

- Content when moving with pets

- Downsizing information

- When to Rent versus When to Buy

- Community videos

- 10 Reasons to Live in Each Town

- Lists of Recommended Vendors

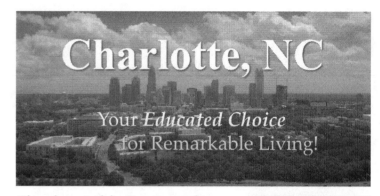

Check out this **Community Video** as if you were new to the State & City. If you would like Ryan and I to help you produce your own: ryanthedesigner@gmail.com (note: active QR code)

Reach out to all **Relo directors** and human resource directors with your Relo packet and send them a copy of your **community video** – as out-of-area Buyers especially appreciate both community videos and virtual tours of **neighborhoods and homes.**

In another segment (regarding Relo Buyers), we will discuss how to attract Buyers moving in from companies.

NOTES

_____

_____

_____

_____

SEGMENT 20

THE COST TO A BUYER WHEN NOT USING A BUYER AGENT

275

"A lawyer who represents themselves has a fool for a client."
– Abraham Lincoln

"A Buyer who represents themselves has a fool for a client."   – Allan Dalton

If one agrees with Abraham Lincoln that even a trained attorney needs an attorney then this might help explain why even the best real estate agents, when they move out of an area, retain another real estate agent.

How then would one logically conclude that if **a real estate agent needs a Buyer Agent** why would a "lay-person Buyer" represent themselves?

Fortunately for both Buyers and Buyer Agents making the case that Buyers need Buyer Agents would merely represent a solution to a problem that does not exist. Buyers "going it alone" is not a problem because Buyers continue, overwhelmingly, to accept their need for Buyer representation.

According to the 2023 NAR report, **89% of Buyers chose an agent when purchasing real estate.**

The reason for this segment – one which examines the cost to a Buyer when not choosing a Buyer Agent – falls to the belief, moving forward, that the greater and negotiated decision for Buyers will not be **whether or not they want Buyer representation** but rather whether to pay for Buyer representation … and if so how much?

This segment is being framed as "What does a Buyer lose" or **how it might cost them by not paying for representation.**

Often, the pain of losing something can be even more impactful and meaningful than the benefits derived from having it. Indeed the perceived loss can be more compelling than the desired gain!

For example, the consequences of a dubious diet or the avoidance of exercise can be more motivational than the benefits of healthy eating and exercise.

Before reviewing some examples of what **can be lost** by Buyers not having a Buyer Agent, please list which major benefits you believe you provide Buyers. This way this subject can be addressed both from the perspective of what is "gained" as well as "the cost of what is lost" by not having a Buyer Agent.

How do you benefit your Buyer Clients?

1 _____   6 _____

2 _____   7 _____

3 _____   8 _____

4 _____   9 _____

5 _____   10 _____

What percentage of Buyers do you think (or would you guess) actually understand or appreciate the value a Buyer Agent provides a Buyer?

10 %   20 %   30 %   40 %   50 %   60 %   70 %   80 %   90 %   100 %

How many of your above-mentioned **Buyer benefits** do you present to your Buyer clients before they agree to your representation?

_____

How many of your **Buyer benefits** are included in your Buyer Agent materials?

_____

What do you believe are the **three greatest Buyer value benefits** you provide?

1 _____

2 _____

3 _____

Suggested examples of how a Buyer is potentially penalized by a lack of professional, knowledgeable, and skillful representation:

1) <u>Community Knowledge</u>: Buyers can pay a price by not having the benefit of the Buyer Agent's deep knowledge of the community, distinct neighborhoods, schools, special needs, and recreational opportunities.

<u>Reason</u>: 75 % of Buyers (according to research) are willing to compromise on the home they select even more than the community. If the Buyer simply relies on their own generic research to learn more about the town and communities they have an interest in without accessing the deeper lifestyle and nuanced knowledge of the realtor, could adversely affect their decision-making.

2) <u>Negotiations</u>:
   Buyers can pay a price by not having a Buyer Agent negotiate for them.

<u>Reason</u>:

Buyers who are new to an area might overpay when they are moving from a much higher-priced region of not represented.

Buyers (if they directly engage with a Home Seller without a Buyer Agent) can suffer because follow-up interest may be considered and exploited as representing over-anxiousness and not part of the normal back-and-forth between agents.

Buyers can become overly personal and confrontational whereas the potential animosity that can occur between parties in a negotiation can be much better managed by an agent.

3) <u>Knowledge of Construction</u>: Buyers can pay a price due to their not routinely assessing the relative merits of construction and a lack of overall construction knowledge.

<u>Reason</u>:

Because Buyers do not see hundreds of thousands of homes, as agents do, they can either overestimate or underestimate the quality of construction and building materials. Also, most Buyers do not have the same level of knowledge of the potential resale value of what and where they are buying.

Buyers are less likely to know what other Buyers think about the construction and may not be familiar with the reputation of local builders.

4) Disclosure:

Buyers can pay a price through a lack of disclosure interpretation.

Reason:

All agents have proclaimed, "No home is perfect!" Therefore, a vital role of a Buyer Agent is their ability to contextualize and place in perspective all disclosure-related issues.

It is vital that Buyers rely upon a real estate trusted advisor who can accurately and objectively put into perspective what each disclosure means for their Buyer in terms of:

a) Present value of the property

b) Future impact on maintenance and home improvement costs

c) Safety issues

d) Resale value

Not having representation in this regard can become monumentally costly.

5) Appraisals: Buyers can pay a price due to their not routinely assessing the relative merits of construction and a lack of overall construction knowledge.

Reason: Appraisals and home inspections need objective interpretation and require context. Since a Buyer's fiduciary agent looks at all reports as if they were buying the property themselves, this means that they are able to explain the appraisal and inspection reports from a knowledgeable real estate perspective. Such experiential knowledge includes a unique understanding of present estimated value, resale value, and how to effectively negotiate inspection items when necessary.

6) <u>Family and pet-related decisions</u>: Buyers need vital counsel from Buyer Agents regarding lifestyle factors related to (when applicable) their children and pets.

Reason:

Real Estate Trusted Advisors who present focused content regarding moving with children and/or pets showcase their deep experiential knowledge of how each community relates to the needs of children and pets.

7) <u>Multiple Offers</u>: Many Buyers become penalized by not having an agent who can optimize the likelihood of winning a multiple-offer transaction.

Reason:

Experienced Buyer Agents, in negotiating multiple offers, devise strategies for their clients and can critically apprise their clients of when their desire to have the home no longer equates to what the multiple offer pricing expectations have reached.

This process, however, must always leave the final negotiating and home selection decision to their Buyer Client. Also, a Buyer Agent can address the question of, "Should we buy before we sell or sell before we buy," along with establishing Buyer purchasing power (qualifying Buyers) regarding either option or the need for bridge financing.

8) <u>When Buyers are out of town</u>: Buyer Agents can continue to search and preview properties on behalf of their clients so they do not lose out.

Reason:

The right home might be the one that Buyers only get to see by their Buyer Agent taking a virtual tour on their behalf.

9) <u>Mortgage, title, and insurance recommendations</u>:
   Buyers lose when they are not guaranteed trusted advice.

<u>Reason</u>:

Buyers benefit by accessing the trusted referrals and the leverage Buyer Agents have that ensures that service providers must do their best to guarantee future referral business ... not only from Buyer Agents but also their brokerages.

10) <u>Co-Broke experience</u>:
    Buyers can lose when there is only one-sided representation.

<u>Reason</u>:

Buyer Agents ensure that the desires, needs, interests, and capabilities of their Buyer Clients are consistently and constantly protected throughout the transaction process.

Successful Buyer Agents have developed enviable reputations amongst community Seller Agents for their professionalism and how they serve as emotional buffers on behalf of their Clients throughout a complex and highly charged transactional process, which are predicates for successful outcomes.

THINGS TO EITHER INDIVIDUALLY CONSIDER OR DISCUSS WITHIN A GROUP

Do you believe a Buyer will be at a disadvantage if they do not have access to a Buyer Agent with knowledge and experience in the following?

1) Community Knowledge   YES   NO

2) Negotiations   YES   NO

3) Knowledge of Construction   YES   NO

4) Disclosure   YES   NO

5) Appraisals   YES   NO

6) Family and pet-related decisions   YES   NO

7) Multiple Offers   YES   NO

8) When Buyers are out of town   YES   NO

9) Mortgage, title, and insurance recommendations   YES   NO

10) Co-Broke experience   YES   NO

Additional Questions

1) How many of the aforementioned benefits do you provide? _____

2) What do you additionally provide?

_____

_____

3) How many of these services do you discuss during your Buyer presentation? _____

4) How many benefits do you think you can guarantee? _____

5) Do you provide Buyers with either a digital or printed outline of all that you do for them?

YES   NO

6) Do you think it will become more important to explain all of your services to Buyers when negotiating fees than in the past when the Buyer did not directly pay a fee?

YES   NO

HERE ARE MY NOTES:

During the 2008 real estate crash, every other stakeholder in a real estate transaction was widely faulted: mortgage companies, government agencies, and credit bureaus. Why? Because the real estate industry is seen as responsible for **facilitating** and not stimulating transactions, therefore appearing feckless and **less valuable or indispensable**.

So too, unless the industry dedicates more attention to educating Clients through predictive data, here again, there is **less value** and Clients are not as able to more judiciously time their investments. Therefore, experiencing major costs by not having represenation.

NOTES

_____

_____

_____

_____

_____

_____

_____

_____

_____

SEGMENT 21
CONVERTING CLIENTS INTO BUYERS

Almost every real estate transaction consists of two sides. This dynamic generally calls for the **involvement or representation of two real estate agents**, unless there is a dual agency situation with only one real estate professional involved. In a small percentage of transactions, there are <u>no real estate professionals included</u>. Indeed, very few real estate transactions occur without representation unlike many other consumer purchases. For example, it would be quite infrequent for a Buyer of an automobile, boat, or swimming pool to have a **fiduciary or trusted advisor** representing their interests in the sales transaction.

In real estate, however, due to each side of the transaction being represented, there exists an industry-wide and massive tendency to view parties in real estate transactions (as well as the potential Client participants in a transaction) as either Buyer or Seller Clients. This **binary delineation** distinctly separates Buyers and Sellers. This is why the real estate industry treats the entire macro-universe of real estate consumers as **placed in one of two categories**. Such compartmentalized consumers become either Buyer or Seller prospects as opposed to being viewed as, first and foremost, all-encompassing real estate Clients. When a real estate consumer's value is narrowly defined as being either a Buyer or a Seller, it **leads to the following phenomenon:**

When a real estate transaction is concluded, either the Buyer Client or Seller Client is relegated to the limited definition of being a 'Past Client'. Essentially, since their side of the transaction was represented (and they therefore are no longer either a Buyer or a Seller Client), they are then universally categorized and their **importance is immediately diminished**.

In this segment I would like to focus on the relationship between this transformational concept and its relationship to **converting Past Clients into Clients for life**... and then into **Buyer Clients**. To fully grasp what I will cover in this program requires an appreciation for how the term 'Client' has been routinely applied in real estate. Generally speaking, the real estate industry has almost exclusively applied the term 'Client' to define the professional relationship that occurs solely during the process of buying or selling of real estate. Specifically, the Client relationship begins with the first substantive meeting in which the **agency relationship is disclosed and accepted** through the consummation and closing of the real estate transaction. This limited and parenthetical use of the word 'Client' is in use only during the real estate transaction process. The term 'Client' is not extended relationally over years and its omission is the predicate for the widely accepted terms 'Past Clients' and 'databases' versus 'Clients for life' and 'Client bases'. As a result of this narrow definition (unlike how a patient can remain a Client of a psychiatrist for many years and not just during episodic treatments) has also led to real estate agents being educated and coached in the following way... They are educated and coached to treat their business as 'a business' versus a 'professional practice'.

The consequences of how all of these terms (which emanate from how a Client is defined as being exclusively transactional and not relational) has **caused many real estate professionals to overlook how businesses have sporadic customers whereas professional practices develop and retain Clients for Life.**

This limited definition of 'Client' (and specifically Buyer and Seller Clients as opposed to real estate Clients in general) has led the industry to either prospect or pay for leads in order to secure either 'Buyer' or 'Seller leads'... as opposed to **all-encompassing 'real estate leads'.**

The purpose of this segment is to **rethink this longstanding real estate paradigm regarding how Clients are defined.** Logic would suggest that rather than seeking to choose to cultivate merely either 'potential Buyer or Seller Clients' independently (by attempting to time when that particular need arises), instead one should seek Clients that might be interested in 'either side' or potentially interested in 'both sides' of the transaction.

Think about it, how much extra effort would it take, instead of advertising to homeowners with a "When you're looking to sell" ad to instead create one that states: "If you're looking to sell, buy, or enhance your home... give me a call!" **Even this revised appeal is limited** as it confirms that you are still prospecting for Clients instead of following up with Clients. This can become your mindset when you appreciate that homeowners are not required to have either bought or sold a home from you in the Past for them to now view you as **their real estate agent** and they as **your immediate Clients**.

In order to optimize one's pursuit of **potential and undeclared real estate Clients**, one must contemplate the consequences of the following:

- That one can **retain Clients before and after a transaction** and never allow them to become diminished as **'Past Clients'**.

- That one can create Clients who have never had a transaction with you or never will but who can become a source of **Client-generated referrals**.

- That one can work in a state like Florida (where some agents serve as transactional facilitators and where their Buyers and Sellers are not their Clients during the transaction), where they can **create Client relationships during non-transactional periods**.

In order to transform one's approach from focusing on 'Past Clients' to 'Clients for life' and from only focusing on 'two micros' (Buyers or Sellers) to one macro: 'real estate Clients' requires a strategy, resources, education (partially provided here), having a coach on the same page, and your personal commitment to "becoming indispensible!"

STRATEGIES TO CREATE BUYER CLIENTS THROUGH YOUR VERSION OF PROVIDING REAL ESTATE TRUSTED ADVICE FOR LIFE

- Create public seminars or Zoom meetings for Buyers. Since available marketing and educational materials include the following resources, this empowers you to produce comprehensive buying side events.

- How to Downsize

- How to Move up

- How to Become a First-Time Buyer

- How to increase the value of home purchases or make suitable modifications

- You can also invite select vendors to help sponsor and speak

- Bring your version of a real estate or real estate financial planning guide to open houses. These should not treat consumers as either a 'Buyer' or a 'Seller', but as 'prospective real estate Clients' who, over their lifetime, need to traverse both sides of the transaction and, at times, simultaneously.

- It makes more sense to have a 'Client for life' if you can offer a service that does not simply rely upon transactional or merely home maintenance needs but rather provides an ongoing advisory relationship.

- In the segment on 'leveraging supported vendors', we cover how to maximize all of these relationships with Buyers, specifically, and Clients in general.

- You should consider saying, to every adult who approaches you regarding real estate, the following, either... "I've been looking forward to asking you to become one of my real estate Clients," or, "I would love for you to become one of my real estate Clients. There is no cost to you and I would like to explain how I serve my clients."

DISCUSSION POINTS

1) Have you ever used the term "my Past Clients"?   YES   NO

2) Do you still use that term?   YES   NO

3) What do you think and say instead... if anything?

_____

_____

4) What percentage of Buyers do you think also have a home to sell? _____

5) How do you answer a Buyer who tells you, "In order to buy we must first sell"?

_____

_____

6) How do you answer, "Should we sell before we buy?"

_____

_____

7) What content & marketing do you employ to encourage Home Sellers to buy?

_____

_____

8) Do you bring Buyer materials (not just data) & content to all open houses?

YES   NO

9) Have you done Buyer or real estate planning events?

YES   NO

DISCUSSION POINTS (Cont.)

10) How do you get and or buy Buyer leads?

_____

_____

11) List your top five sources of Buyers. List all potential sources of Buyers.

_____   _____

_____   _____

_____   _____

_____   _____

12) Which are the most important resources for securing Buyers?

_____

_____

_____

13) What % of your time is devoted to working w/ Buyers vs. Sellers? _____

14) Are you better at working with Buyers or Sellers? _____

15) What % of Buyers do you refer to another agent to work your market? _____

16) What % of your Client base have you provided your version of a
    real estate financial planning guide? _____

SUMMARY

How many consumers think they only have a personal doctor when they have a pressing medical need?

How many people believe the only time they are a Client of their dentist is during an occasional toothache?

How many people think that they are only a Client of their financial planner when they sit down together or file their taxes?

The fact that a homeowner can live in a community for 10–13 years and then, when deciding to move, bring in a **complete real estate stranger** is perhaps the single greatest indictment and consequence of the term 'Past Client' and the need for real estate and financial planning.

Considering how much time, effort, and expense is devoted to securing that one transactional Client, it is inexplicable why there isn't greater effort in converting them into Clients for life based upon real estate planning... along with the deliverance of **ecosystem services** and **support exists as the monumental void that it is**.

NOTES

SEGMENT 22

YOU DON'T NEED TO BE A REAL ESTATE PSYCHIC TO LEVERAGE PREDICTIVE DATA

295

The terms "predictive data" and "predictive analytics" mean precisely what it says: "Data that can predict outcomes and the analysis of predictive data." Not as clear are all the ways predictive data, powered by AI, applies to real estate decision-making. Also unclear are all the ways predictive data plays a role in working with and for real estate Buyers.

The first time I became familiar with the term "predictive data" was twenty years ago when my engineers at Realtor.com told me, "Allan we can predict which types of Homes will sell faster based upon the click behavior of visitors to the site."

This knowledge inspired me to create a campaign for Move Inc. that I named 'Where, When, and How to Move'. The thinking was that (through the use of predictive data) Move Inc. could help realtors better understand the "when" and "where" and the Realtors® would take care of the "how"! This thinking preceded the "artificial intelligence movement" becoming so common within the business vernacular.

Today, due to artificial intelligence delivered through machine learning algorithms, many companies (including CRMSs to varying degrees) are making the following predictions:

- Which homeowners in certain communities will be selling in the next year or two

- Which compositions of households are more likely to move before others

- Where people will move to and from.

- Geographical heat maps predicting both movement and appreciation or deprecation likely levels

• Which floor plans, appliances, properties, towns, and neighborhoods are trending as more desirable

The compilation and combination of historical data, economic indicators, climate, and overall market trends, and predictive analysis is beginning to transform investment analysis, property valuation, and risk assessment.

Therefore it is highly recommended that you conduct a basic Google search surrounding 'real estate AI and predictive data,' 'predictive analysis software programs and companies' to learn the following:

a) How to access this information

b) Learn the Pros and Cons of predictive data

c) How to use and how to misuse

d) How their CRM uses predictive data

e) How to use and introduce to both Buyers and Sellers

Just as economists (who all have access to similar data) arrive at many different cities' conclusions, so too this will be the result in real estate... as there are many potential data points that are not predictable with absolute certainty. Remember the term is predictive data and not guaranteed data. Fortunes have been lost in both the stock market and real estate based upon overreliance on predictive data. Yet, fortunes have also been made by the prudent analysis of data.

You cannot ethically make predictions as to how much a home or market will appreciate. Predictive data does not guarantee the future.

What predictive data does provide is the best possible assessment of what might happen in the future.

Your Best Uses of Predictive Data

To inform your off and online marketing strategy it can:

a) Help you triage which households are more important to market to

b) Shrink your budget by eliminating predictable waste that occurs by misguided marketing to the wrong prospects

c) Improve your ROI

d) Help you match content by identifying nuances within markets and consumers

As an example:

Moving with children and pets to the more predictive homes and neighborhoods where this is relevant.

Downsizing (you can learn which neighborhoods are better candidates) and use Chalk Digital to send out downsizing content links. Send those homeowners, whom predictive data indicates are more likely to be selling, information that positions you as the right agent to select.

Questions

What are the most important predictive data points that you should market or discuss with Home Sellers?

1. _____

2. _____

3. _____

4. _____

5. _____

What are the most important predictive data points you should share with Buyers?

1. _____

2. _____

3. _____

4. _____

5. _____

Questions (Cont.)

List which sources you will use for predictive data:

1. _____

2. _____

3. _____

4. _____

5. _____

How and when should predictive data not be used?

_____

_____

_____

_____

Questions (Cont.)

Which areas of predictive data do you believe will have the greatest impact upon the real estate industry?

1. _____

2. _____

3. _____

4. _____

5. _____

Will predictive data increase, decrease, or have no impact on your perceived value?

_____

Do you think predictive data will be more helpful with:

Buyers	YES	NO
Sellers	YES	NO
Home Sellers	YES	NO

NOTES

SEGMENT 23

REBHAN ON RELO

An Interview with Relocation Specialist, Kathleen Rebhan

Relo and Out-of-Area Buyers are significant segments of the overall Buyer pool. One of the benefits of creating your digital version of The 7 A's of Buyer Agent Representation is that it establishes your Value immediately.

Kathleen Rebhan has devoted decades of her professional career to elevating Service and Services to so-called Relo Buyers and enhancing the Value and Skills of Buyer Agents!

DALTON:
What do Relo companies look for in who they select?

REBHAN:
Experience, reputation, location, specialized training, credentials, memberships in RDC, ERC, and local boards.

DALTON:
Why is Relo not for everyone?

REBHAN:
Expensive, continued training and membership fees with professional associations are required as well as the ability to absorb the cost(s) to maintain inventory property until closing. This requires a very good accounting of expenses too. An in-house tracking system for the placement and tracking is important to have and maintain.

DALTON:
What do Relo agents have to know that other agents might not?

REBHAN:
Relo agents understand the timing and emotional impact of the relocation process. They are experts in the area they represent including school districts and private schools, commuting routes, local tax implications, locations of local houses of worship, and other opportunities-information not necessarily needed by a local buyer.

DALTON:

Is it worth the referral fee you have to pay?

REBHAN:

You would be correct to assume some agents will not work with a client if there is a referral fee but most know this will be guaranteed business- the relocated employee has to move. It is also better to earn a percent of a fee than to receive no fee at all.

DALTON:

How much more paperwork is involved?

REBHAN:

Buyer and Seller information requirements are different. Both require some sort of status reporting to the Relocation company and the Seller side requires completion of a specialized form, the "Worldwide ERC® Broker's Market Analysis and Strategy Report" along with photos of the property and the comparable properties. It is not an easy form to complete and it is time-consuming.

DALTON:

Is it easier to work with Relo departments or HR?

REBHAN:

I don't know we never work with HR directly.

DALTON:

Does the Relo company ever pay the buying side fee?

REBHAN:

Occasionally if not offered by the Seller and occasionally for a lease situation when no compensation is offered.

DALTON:

Do you think this percentage will increase?

REBHAN:

Will have to see what happens with all of the compensation lawsuits currently being brought forth. They may have to in order for their transferees to be represented in their transactions.

DALTON:

How do you counsel Relo buyers?

REBHAN:

We start by informing them of the local customs in real estate, i.e. "How to buy a house in Charlotte!" Then move to commute times from various areas to their new work location. After that, there is a discussion of price, style, age, etc. as with a traditional buyer.

DALTON:

What percentage of Relo buyers have families versus individuals?

REBHAN:

I'm not sure where to find this particular statistic but I would say 80% of our relocation buyers have been families.

DALTON:

What do you include in your Relo package?

REBHAN:

Our **Welcome to Charlotte** video, property listings, maps, links to local news sources, state association, sample forms/contracts, information on local sports teams, and recreational facilities especially if the transferee has asked about these things.

DALTON:

Do sellers think Relo buyers should be able to pay more?

REBHAN:

No, they welcome their urgency.

DALTON:

How do you become the go-to Relo buyer to corporations?

REBHAN:

Professionalism, Credentials, Past successful experiences, and our favorite... **to be referred by Relocated employees**. We also keep abreast of the changes in corporate offices in the area and contact them to offer our services when having a corporate move.. both in and out of the area.

DALTON:

What do you have to do for Relo buyers that you do not do for other buyers?

REBHAN:

More contact when they come to town. Local buyers do not expect a continuous four (or more days) of an agent's time to look at and choose their next home.

DALTON:

Do you have a Relo questionnaire?

REBHAN:

No, our experience is that a conversation with each individual relocating employee is more important to earn their trust and increase their confidence in the move.

DALTON:

How do you keep the corporation updated?

REBHAN:

However they want us to. Most today have an established system for reporting. The update is completed by the agent, reviewed by our in-house relocation manager, and then forwarded to the relocation company.

DALTON:

How do you arrange to refer a Relo buyer to another part of your market you are familiar with?

REBHAN:

You don't! If a relocation buyer wants to move to a different location, they must go back to the relocation company and request it. Only "within company" transfers are possible without approval from the Relocation Company. Our relocation manager will explain the situation and often suggests another company if possible.

DALTON:

How much information do you receive from their Relo or HR department about the buyer?

REBHAN:

Basic information: name, address, phone, current address, and email are always supplied. Occasionally we are also provided with other family members and their ages, locations they have pre-selected, price range, and move date.

DALTON:
is any of the info confidential?

REBHAN:
Yes, especially on a government move.

DALTON:
As a Relo buyer agent, do you have ethical limits as to what you can share back to the company?

REBHAN:
No, the Relocation company needs to be aware of anything that will impact the corporate clients' expectations of getting the employees to the location where they are needed.

DALTON:
Thank you so much for all this, Kathy!

REBHAN:
My pleasure, Allan!

———————— ❧ ————————

Should you have any additional questions regarding Relocation, feel free to connect with Kathleen at KRebhan@bhhselite.com

SEGMENT 24

PREPARING YOUR BROKERAGE FOR GREATER BUYING SIDE VALUE

An Interview with Emmett Laffey
CEO of BHHS Laffey, Filmore and Montauk

A word about Emmett Laffey:

Emmett Laffey is a highly respected Metropolitan New York Broker Owner and his 50-year anniversary brokerage has regional sales and marketing centers located throughout Brooklyn, Queens, and Long Island. This Manhattan to Montauk real estate juggernaut is especially noted for its innovativeness, career development systems, and dominance within the luxury market.

●┈┈┈┈┈┈┈┈┈┈┈┈┈┈┈┈┈┈┈●

DALTON: Emmett, it is certainly no secret that brokerages throughout the industry are significantly focused on the necessary changes they must make to effectively adapt to a post-disrupted real estate world. While this book is overwhelmingly focused on providing suggestions from team leaders and agents, I would be remiss not to also include recommendations from a leading and highly respected brokerage owner. What are you doing to prepare for these transformational changes and also could you share the markets you serve?

EMMETT: Our company has offices from Manhattan to Montauk by virtue of our many great locations throughout Brooklyn, Queens, and Long Island. Regarding our preparations, each Wednesday we have an 'all-hands-on-deck company-wide meeting'. That title best explains our company's overall approach to preparing for changes and now includes how our Buyer Agents must present their negotiated value to prospective Buyer Clients moving forward.

DALTON: What does an 'all-hands-on-deck company-wide movement' look like?

EMMETT: It began by explaining and discussing with all of our managers, agents, and teams that, due to how people struggle with changes, 25-50% of real estate agents will not be able to adapt. Clearly, there will now be a significant percentage of agents who will be demoralized...

EMMETT (CONT.): ... and overwhelmed by the order of magnitude caused by this unexpected predicament, one which will require significant greater emphasis on compensated buyer side value. This means there will be even greater opportunities for agents who evolve in response to these different real estate policies, circumstances and buyer expectations.

DALTON: What do you think will specifically cause some agents to leave the industry?

EMMETT: Changes to the status quo and an inability for real estate agents to shift from where Buyers were not asked to pay fees to where they will now be asked to directly compensate our Buyer Agents.

DALTON: You told me that you have had agents who have, for years, represented Buyers and agree, in advance of a sale, to pay a Buyer Agent a fee. What percentage of the Buyer Agents both in your company and beyond would you estimate were consistently paid by the buyer?

EMMETT: I would estimate that less than 2% were routinely compensated by the Buyer Client!

DALTON: Is it your plan to include these agents who have developed the ability to convince Buyers of their Buying-side representational value, leading to a compensated buyer agreeing to share their experiential knowledge with your company at large?

EMMETT: Yes. I have asked all of our managers to make sure that within their in-office training, education classes, and role-playing exercises, they make sure to blend in the experiences of these agents. I am combining the experience of our best Buyer Agents who did not receive compensation from the Buyer, along with those who did, and our new '7 A's of Buyer Agent Value presentation'. This is the only way to effectively respond to this newly introduced and somewhat unexpected need... and again, with an 'all-hands-on-deck approach' to maximize our preparation.

DALTON: I am assuming that since you have consented to my interview request you are willing to share, if not all of the particulars, at least some of the broad strokes regarding these newly introduced concepts that you have introduced at your major Metro New York regional brokerage?

EMMETT: I am happy to share information that can be helpful to other brokerages, especially concepts that help them to possibly bring greater value to Buyers. While we cannot ever make suggestions regarding what fees any other companies should charge as they negotiate fees with either Sellers or Buyers, I am very comfortable sharing business strategies just as I benefit in return from broker-sharing groups.

DALTON: Thank you for that. What are you doing specifically that might help some other brokerages?

EMMETT: After weeks and months of research, by testing potential programs and solutions at our all-hands-on-deck collaborative and company-wide meetings, I made the decision to first produce and then present to the company three programs that are integrated as one three-dimensional Buyer-side service. Those three are our company-branded Home Buying System, Guaranteed Buyer Program, and the 7 A's of Buyer Representation Value Presentation and its collateral materials.

DALTON: First, why was it so important to involve your entire company in this educational and creative process?

EMMETT: This year we celebrated our fiftieth anniversary. When I was recently asked how I explained such sustained success I cited four major reasons: great salespeople, great managers, great at listing properties. and complete transparency!

Transparency means everything to me, it is a great passion of mine and I insist that transparency be a part of everything our company does or is thinking of doing. Transparency to me also means constant dialogue and interaction. This is why all of our education must be interactive and not lecture-style.

DALTON: Why a Buyer's Guarantee? What are you guaranteeing?

EMMETT: No one can guarantee a Buyer how much they will pay or how long the buying process will take. What can be guaranteed is the process or overall framework... one that we teach and expect our Buyer Agents to deliver. I think of it as similar to a patient's bill of rights. This is where hospitals guarantee a fundamental number of procedures that each patient is entitled to and will receive.

DALTON: How do you explain your Buyer Guarantee to your agents?

EMMETT: Very clearly. I explain, and my entire company agrees, that each Buyer who relies upon one of our Buyer Agents at the very least deserves a consistent level of representation, instead of a hit-and-miss. An Apple iPhone, a certain model of automobile, and even a Big Mac must provide everyone with a similar value. Of course, just as someone can purchase upgrades when buying an automobile, this is also how individual Buyer Agents in our company can then further customize and personalize our fundamental Buyer-side Value. If I can not provide this consistency for both my agents and consumers then we are a holding company without a company culture. This is also why I created the Listing Guarantee.

DALTON: How did you select your Buying-side's fundamental and basic value, not only so you could realistically guarantee its delivery, but also so your Buyer Agents can insert their personal value and add their extras?

EMMETT: Allan, that's a leading question. As you know, through the **7 A's of Buyer Agent Value** we cover all of the fundamentals regarding the value of representation and ones that are both basic and realistic yet where our Buyer Agents are completely comfortable guaranteeing such comprehensive representation. The key is that these points of value are all easy for folks to understand and begin with the same letter... that being 'A'.

EMMETT: We have been coaching our agents on The 7 A's of Buyer Agent Value and our Buyer Agents appreciate that while this methodology provides easy-to-follow clarity for Buyers, that is up to our Buyer Agents to individualize and customize what each of the seven areas of value represents, based on their experience and personal style of communication.

Allan, thank you for launching 'The 7 A's' here in the Big Apple!

DALTON: What has the response to this easy-to-follow and step-by-step building block process?

EMMETT: Absolutely positive! We have very sophisticated agents, as you would expect in the New York area. They appreciate that just as home sellers want to be convinced of a Seller Agent's Value before they accept a negotiated fee, so too when Buyers realize that they will also be expected to pay a fee (and for most the first time), they will also need to be 'sold' first.

DALTON: I recently coined the Acronym 'FBBO' – a category of consumers who, unlike for sale by owners, wish to be For Buyer By Owners! Given how some Buyers might conclude that they can find homes online, visit open houses unescorted, and arrange for financing, inspections, and appraisals, how important do you think it is for Buyer Agents to stress even greater and irreplaceable value than in the past?

EMMETT: It is vitally important given the new policies regarding where compensation comes from! Thankfully we are a full-service company. More than ever, as mentioned, we need to show Buyers that we can not only help them buy homes but also with a plan to maximize the home's value after its acquisition...

EMMETT (cont.): ...and benefit from the relationships we have developed with architects, builders, and tradespeople. Also, we can help Buyers establish their purchasing power through our mortgage relationships and professional contacts. When Buyer Agents extend the value of their professional and personal relationships with key real estate-related service providers, it prevents Buyers from having to endure the futility of dealing with 'answering machines'. Allan, because we are in New York, our Clients want things done 'in a New York Minute'. This can only be accomplished through real estate ecosystems led by Buyer Agents. Our strategic mortgage relationships, for example, can help Buyer Clients establish their purchasing power, so with proof of funds, their Buyer Agent can negotiate on their behalf and position them as cash Buyers. We can also help with utility hook-ups, settling-in services, and a wide range of home-related services.

DALTON: Is full service or better yet 'full services' more important or valuable to either Buyers or Sellers?

EMMETT: Not only are 'full services' more valuable to Buyers than Sellers before and during a transaction but they are infinitely more valuable to a Buyer staying in town than leaving. Also, Buyer-side Value, in general, is at least as great as the value we provide Sellers. Buyer representations, frequently and generally, require more work, more time, and the need to develop deeper relationships.

In many cases, relationships have to be formed with more Buyer Partners, friends, and families than on the Selling-side. Buying-side agents require more community knowledge, greater knowledge of construction, more patience, and more information and advice provided with each property being considered. I love that Buyer Agents will now be expected to validate their value more than ever... and now will have two bites of the 'Value Apple'!

DALTON: Congratulations on your company's fiftieth anniversary, Emmett. The ability to flourish for this many decades must have taken a lot more than just 'the Luck of the Irish'!

Should you have any additional questions, feel free to connect with Emmett at emmett@bhhslaffey.com

SEGMENT 25
THE CHANGING BUYERS LANDSCAPE

Real estate brokers and agents across the globe have been known to proclaim, "Our market is different!" A refrain perhaps more important but less said is, "Real estate is different from any other consumer or Client-centric experience." If more focus from within the industry had been devoted to the reality that the way real estate professionals engage and serve the consumer is very different then perhaps the need to **fully represent Buyers** and to be **directly compensated** would have occurred decades sooner.

While real estate laws and ethics are either largely governed or advanced by states and the National Association of Realtors®, ethos is the domain of brands and brokerages.

Ethics is what one must do.
Ethos is what one should also do... even beyond ethics.

Just a few decades ago (and for many years prior) most real estate agents working with a Buyer were sub-agents to the Home Seller... <u>even though most Buyers were not aware of this practice</u>.

In more recent times, this practice of conventional sub-agency (where only the Seller had full representation) was changed in most of America. Now in 2024 and beyond there will be another major transition regarding how home Buyers are to be served. Specifically and increasingly Buyers will be either asked or expect to **pay a fee directly to the Buying-side brokerage**.

Accordingly, the content within this program is intended for **educational and discussion purposes only** and not to either introduce or impose upon any individual brokerage affiliate any policy or edicts regarding their Buyer brokerage practices. It is up to each brokerage to decide what their business policies are as long as they're in compliance with state and Federal laws.

In order for brokerages to **determine and then develop their particular buying side value** it is helpful to begin, to the degree possible, to place themselves in the so-called shoes of Buyers. If you were not in real estate and looking to buy a home/lifestyle, how do you think you would respond to the following questions?

Each question calls for a simple yes, no, or uncertain response:

1) As a Buyer, I would expect that I would not have to pay a fee/commission to the agent working with or representing me.

YES   NO   UNCERTAIN

2) I might think that my agent was more interested in **making a sale** than doing whatever it took to help me/us find the best home possible for our circumstances and budget.

YES   NO   UNCERTAIN

3) I might think that my agent was less willing to show me properties where they might **not be compensated or compensated less** (new construction, for sale by owner, out of area).

YES   NO   UNCERTAIN

4) I might think that my agent would be more interested in showing me their own listings.

YES   NO   UNCERTAIN

If you answered **yes or uncertain** to any of these questions, your answers can be the basis for either further introspection or group discussion.

For years (and even now) there has been suspicion that Buyer Agents – as is the case with all commission-compensated agents – are not solely acting in the complete interests of the Buyer or purchaser... as many agents represent a **win-win philosophy** when it comes to negotiations... unlike other fiduciaries who only aggressively look out for the interests of their Clients.

This is why all previous segments in this book addressed:

1) How to win the trust and confidence of Buyers.

2) Optimizing value in light of present-day Buyer concerns by focusing on:

a) How to optimize the value of data

b) How to guide Buyers on best search practices

c) How to introduce your negotiation value

d) How to present a Buyer's guarantee

e) The importance of confidentiality

f) Legal compliance and due diligence

g) Transactional support

h) Post-sale services

i) Real estate planning

This segment began by stating that **real estate is different** let it conclude by identifying how so and its many implications. When most purchasers buy stocks, bonds, boats, new home construction through the developer, and automobiles... there is only one professional typically involved. This means clarity regarding representation.

The auto salesperson is representing the dealership.
The on-site salesperson working for the developer represents the builder.

Yet in real estate, **there are two sides to each transaction**. In the majority, two different agents... in some cases, one agent working with but not fully representing either side... and in most cases, an agent representing each side separately.

This confusion (that can result from this complexity) is not the doing of any brokerage, agent, and certainly not any brand... as brands do not represent Buyers and Sellers. **Everyone in the real estate industry involuntarily inherited this environment.**

This environment has **and will continue to change rapidly**... and this will be for the better!

1) A more comprehensively educated and informed Buyer (and Seller) will develop greater respect for the high-level professionalism of real estate agents.

2) The more Sellers and Buyers pay separately, the negotiated fee they choose, and the agent they select, the more each side of the transaction will appreciate the commensurate skills required for 'both' Buyer and Seller Agents.

3) The more transparency and scrutiny that occurs when both Buyers and Sellers get to assess the relative value of their individual agents – on each side of the transaction – the more real estate professionals will be challenged to continue to evolve and develop their core competency.

4) The more that each side has to be equally satisfied regarding the worth and value of their agent **in relationship to the fees they pay** the more your values and your brokerage's values become relevant.

The purpose of this segment is to **rethink this longstanding real estate paradigm regarding how Clients are defined.** Logic would suggest that rather than seeking to choose to cultivate merely either 'potential Buyer or Seller Clients' independently (by attempting to time when that particular need arises), instead one should seek Clients that might be interested in all potential real estate options moving forward regardless of their current circumstances.

Think about it, how much extra effort would it take, instead of advertising to homeowners with a "When you're looking to sell" post to instead create one that states: "If you're looking to sell, buy, or enhance your home... give me a call!" **Even this revised appeal is limited** as it confirms that you are still prospecting for Clients instead of following up with Clients. This can become your mindset when you appreciate that homeowners are not required to have either bought or sold a home from you in the past as they now view you as **their real estate agent** and they as **your immediate Clients**.

In order to optimize one's pursuit of **potential and undeclared real estate Clients**, one must contemplate the consequences of the following:

- That one can **retain Clients before and after a transaction** and never allow them to become diminished as **'Past Clients'**.

- That one can create Clients who have never had a transaction with you or never will but who can become a source of **Client-generated referrals**.

- That one can work in a state like Florida (where some agents serve as transactional facilitators and where their Buyers and Sellers are not their Clients during the transaction), yet where they can **create Client relationships during non-transactional periods**.

In order to transform one's approach from focusing on 'Past Clients' to 'Clients for life' and from only focusing on 'two micros' (Buyers or Sellers) to one macro: 'real estate Clients' requires a strategy, resources, education, having a coach on the same page, your personal commitment to become invaluable, and of course continuing to use **Buyer Agent Be Aware** as a continuing resource.

NOTES

SEGMENT 26

EFFECTIVE CO-BROKERAGE

Real estate attracts so-called "People People." Thank goodness because very few transactions are ever consummated, professionally speaking, unilaterally. Yet Top Producers thrive in an industry where they consistently and simultaneously **cooperate and compete**.

I recently, in preparation for my report, called upon some of the leading producers in the industry to learn what they believe are the keys to successful co-brokering. While hardly earth-shattering, the information offered is an important reminder of how to conduct oneself most professionally and respectfully... **while at the same time remaining a staunch advocate as a fiduciary for your Buyer Clients.**

It's all about the relationship!

- Know the agent already ... from attending as many brokers opens, events, networking and public opens, following up, and communicating well in past deals.

- With a respectful, considerate tone, call the agent before showing:

    - If representing the Buyer, tell them a bit about your Buyer and ask if there is anything you should know about the home or the Seller.

    - If representing the Seller, call the agent to thank them for the future showing, share info that you want to share about the Seller, and ask about the Buyer.

- When showing, compliment the agent in front of their Clients, when and if possible but don't overdo it.

COMMUNICATE effectively. Provide feedback ASAP. Be as specific as you can. NEVER JUST SAY, "It wasn't for them." Give them specifics.

- Send a thank you card with a "little something" to the co-agent: a gift card, chocolate bar, or something small after closing.

- Call / text agents you admire when they get a new listing or close a deal just to congratulate them. This will build relationships.

- Do not overprotect your Client. Discuss your strategy for buying in this market. If there aren't multiple offers, start with a number closer to where you want to end up versus leaving more room for negotiation: the first number being closer gives the co-broker something to work with and they will not be tempted to use words "like bottom feeder" which starts the negotiation off in the wrong direction ... and puts the co-broker in a place where they are more prone to bad behavior. The first number makes a difference in low inventory markets, especially with both Client and agent!

- WORK together! This is not done enough. Discuss the negotiation and what is important to both parties so they feel collaboration.

- NEVER say, "You do know this is overpriced," or, "You know it needs to be totally renovated," or, "It's on a bad road," etc. Co-brokers will get defensive and it starts the ball rolling in the wrong way. YES, you can point things out but do so respectfully in conversation. You know they absolutely love the property and they are excited to make it their own. "They have to budget for the roof and new furnace, so we are bringing in an offer of _____."

- Pay attention to detail when presenting an offer. Send EVERYTHING at once in a concise full offer with everything they need. Always write a letter to the agent and suggest they share with their Clients.

- Get creative and honor their ideas if they have any ... even if you don't use them, express gratitude for their creativity.

- Be a strong negotiator ... not a bully.

- Refer a reliable attorney, inspector, and mortgage people so that the co-broker can't complain about any of them to their Client
  (THIS IS A BIG ONE!)

The obvious...

- Be respectful

- Be professional

- Be knowledgeable: know your market

- Pick up your phone, answer your emails and texts promptly

- When showing your own property, don't talk too much. Be there to tell the story and answer questions but do not take over. Do not outshine their agent... although this may sometimes be impossible.

———————————— ✳ ————————————

Discussion Points

Please list the 5 most important factors in managing an effective co-brokerage opportunity on behalf of your Buyer Client.

_____   _____

_____   _____

_____   _____

Discussion Points (Cont.)

What is different, if anything, when Buyers are paying Buyer-side fees regarding how you communicate with the Seller Agent?

_____

_____

_____

_____

Will you speak more emphatically to a Buyer who is paying you regarding how you have a fiduciary responsibility to them or will you continue presenting your representational value in the same way as when a Buyer is not paying a fee? Do you agree that it should not make any difference?

_____

_____

_____

_____

NOTES

SEGMENT 27

BUYER AGENT
BE AWARE
FINAL QUIZ

1) Will you develop a Buyer Consultation Presentation
(7 A's or otherwise) and role-play the presentation?   YES   NO

     By When? _____

2) Will you change anything you do regarding Open Houses?   YES   NO

     By When? _____

3) Will you begin to produce a long-form Community Video?   YES   NO

     By When? _____

4) Will you develop a Home Buying System?   YES   NO

     By When? _____

5) Will you change anything you are doing for Luxury Buyers?   YES   NO

     By When? _____

6) Will you make changes to your use of Social Media Marketing?   YES   NO

     By When? _____

7) Will you do a Buyer Seminar?   YES   NO

     By When? _____

8) Will you create more Buyer-side Videos and Content?   YES   NO

     By When? _____

9) Will you prospect for New Construction Listings?   YES   NO

     By When? _____

10) Will you create a Rent to Buy System?　　　　YES　　NO

　　By When? _____

11) Will you research Real Grader?　　　　YES　　NO

　　By When? _____

12) Will you research Chalk Digital?　　　　YES　　NO

　　By When? _____

13) Will you do more with BombBomb?　　　　YES　　NO

　　By When? _____

14) Will you become more of an EDU-salesperson?　　　　YES　　NO

　　By When? _____

15) Will you become a Certified Buyer Agent?　　　　YES　　NO

　　By When? _____

16) Will you provide a buyer MMA　　　　YES　　NO
(an analysis of what can produce future value through home improvements)

　　By When? _____

17) Will you produce a Clients Only Home Services Directory?　　　　YES　　NO

　　By When? _____

18) Will you refer more Mortgage, Title, and Insurance?　　　　YES　　NO
(either your company's or others)

　　By When? _____

AFTERWORD
The Term 'Listing Agent' Threatens
'Buyer Agent' Relevance and Value

Buyer Agent Be Aware, true to its title, has devoted full and exclusive focus to all things 'Buyer Agent'. Yet, since I suspect that the overwhelming percentage of the readers of this work also represent Home Sellers, I want to introduce the following thoughts… thoughts which I candidly think have been completely overlooked by the real estate industry at large:

That being that the manner in which most, or at the very least many Home Seller representatives position their title and essence (Listing Agent) is potentially damaging to Buyer Agents… especially those Buyer Agents who, in many cases, will be seeking to charge direct and negotiated compensation from Buyers for the first and ongoing time, moving forward.

In my travels throughout the country, it appears that many real estate professionals who represent Home Sellers are still being referred to as 'listing agents'. I believe anyone who continues to either advertise or asks, "Who is the listing agent," should cease and desist.

All agents representing Home Sellers should join their colleagues who consistently and unwaveringly refer to Home Seller Agents as 'Sellers Agent'. Especially when a Buyer Client asks a Buyer Agent, "Who is the listing agent," one should say, "The agent representing the homeowner is Jane Doe," as a way of reminding the Buyer Client that the Seller has an agent and therefore they should as well!

Here are reasons why I am suggesting the detonation of the term Listing Agent:

1) **Listing Agent sounds like the agent is representing the listing** or the home… and not their Clients.

2) **Listing Agent is not symmetrical to Buyer Agent.** Accordingly, why should the Buyer Agent title announce Buyer Agency while Listing Agent does not as clearly connote the same relationship to their Client?

3) **The anachronistic term 'Listing Agent'** further encourages Buyers to avoid Buyer Representation. This is because the term Listing Agent sounds more welcoming and less oppositional than Seller Agent. Moreover, since the Listing Agent has the most information on the property and the name sounds equally helpful to Sellers and Buyers, then it suggests that the **'Listing Agent' is where Buyers should start**... and maybe stay to save money.

4) If there is not full and unambiguous value on both sides of the transaction then there can never be exceptional value on either side.

5) Plaintiff's attorneys compel that there must also be defendant attorneys. Very clearly one represents plaintiffs and the other defendants while neither represents the paperwork, the contract, or the so-called 'listing' of their client.

6) When Sellers see that Buyers do not have an agent representing their interests, and one not negotiating for them, it raises this question, "Why then should I have a Seller Agent?" Especially in the age of artificial intelligence and free access to real estate information, Buyers must be provided with more reasons to start with a Buyer Agent and not less. Regrettably, the outdated and value-killing nomenclature **'Listing Agent'** reinforces what might be perceived as a cavalier commitment to agency and one's clients.

Listing Agents may think this is exactly what they want... for Buyers not to appreciate Buyer Agent Value so they will come directly to the Listing Agent. Yet, this can also lead to Sellers concluding, "If I am giving up full negotiation value, then what am I paying for," or, "If Buyers do not require representation, maybe I do not either!" **All value, therefore, on both sides of the transaction risks unraveling!** Also of concern, for some, might be that, again, so-called Listing Agents who seek to become Buyer Agents (on other occasions) are unwittingly confirming the lack of a need for full Buyer Agency Representation... which also disadvantages Buyers by depriving them of full agency representation.

7) Because some learn best through analogies, let me share one: Let's say, instead of referring to those agents who represent Buyers as Buying Agents that Buyers thought they were retaining and compensating 'Showing Agents'. How do you think this would impact the perceived value of a Buyer Agent?

Do the words 'Showing Agents' show as much value as 'Buyer Agents'?
Do the words 'Listing Agent' suggest as much value as 'Selling Agent'?

How did the real estate industry (to the degree that there are rituals) ever get saddled with this lowest possible description of what represents immense real estate Seller Agent Value?

In the 1800s, (before the MLS, IDX, internet, videos, etc., and even newspapers were in vogue) when a homeowner wanted to 'sell their home', there was a board at the local general store that read, "List your home for sale!" Therefore, effectively defining the Home Owner as the 'Listing Agent' by virtue of listing the home for sale on a board! **Perhaps it's time to rethink the importance of words.**

The marketing and networking of homes have come a long way since then... but the definition, relating to value, has not! It would be as though we still called iPhones 'Rotary Phones'. Confucius, in his rectification of names, wrote, "All wisdom begins by properly naming things, and when you don't, kingdoms will fall and dynasties will tumble."

Shakespeare wrote, "Suit the word to the action," in Hamlet. Does anyone truly think the word 'Listing Agent' describes what a Seller Agent does? A 'Seller Agent' can, however, as it would encapsulate everything the Seller Agent does for the Home Seller.

Plato said, "Names should correctly describe the entity," in his Correction of Names thesis. I believe everything should be done within the industry to ensure that consumers are presented with every opportunity to learn and benefit from of the full and unambiguous value of having full representation on either side of the transaction.

In my opinion, if there is not equally perceived value on each side of the transaction (similar to the prosecutor on one side and the defense attorney on the other) then, ultimately, there will be no value. As I say, words matter… and I hope that every Seller Agent and Buyer respectfully agrees. While most of the industry, I believe, is focused on the 'tactical' and forced changes on how offers of compensation (through MLSs) will be treated, my greater focus is on larger and more 'strategic' issues.

For example, how will brokerages and Buyer Agents respond if and when 'Listing Agents' begin to advertise, "Attention, Buyers! You don't need a Buyer Agent to visit my Open House," or, "Attention, Home Sellers! We will not ask you to make any concessions!"

DETAILS MATTER!

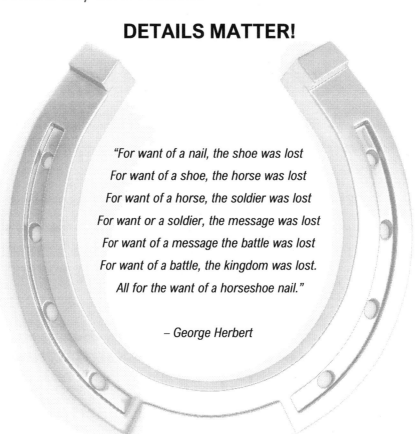

"For want of a nail, the shoe was lost
For want of a shoe, the horse was lost
For want of a horse, the soldier was lost
For want or a soldier, the message was lost
For want of a message the battle was lost
For want of a battle, the kingdom was lost.
All for the want of a horseshoe nail."

– George Herbert

It has been a privilege for me, Ryan Ward, and our seven contributors to produce and provide what we truly believe is the most needed, timely, and topical real estate educational resource ever for the industry and its professionals, whom we deeply respect. If you have found value well in excess of the cost of this book, please spread the word.

– Allan Dalton • allandaltonconsulting@gmail.com

MY 60/40 ACKNOWLEDGMENTS

Here are my 'Top 60' real estate professionals
(listed alphabetically) from the last 40+ years,
who hired, influenced, taught, or caused me to admire them deeply
(or all of the above)

Gary Acosta	Bob Goldberg	Martha Mosier
Candace Adams	Sam Guillen	Joe Murphy
Karen Balter	Gordon Gundaker	Creig Northrop
Ken Baris	Hanna Family	Charlie & Michael Oppler
Bob Becker	Joe Hanauer	Mike Pappas
Gino Blefari	Tom Hart	George Patsio
Christy Budnick	Rick Higgins	Brad Patt
Jean Burgdorff	Michael Jalbert	Craig Proctor
Jimmy Burgess	Sherri Johnson	Bill Raveis
Cristal Clarke	Chris Kelly	Kathy Rehban
Allen Crumbley	Emmet Laffey	Larry Rideout
Barbara Corcoran	Anthony Lamacchia	Dick Schlott
Debbie DeGrote	Will Langley	Teresa Palacios Smith
Steve Fase	Bob LeFever	Kim & Maxwell Stevens
John Featherston	Vince Leisey	Chris Stuart
Mike Ferry	Tyrone Lesley	Andrew Undem
Tom Ferry	Dave Liniger	Julie Vanderblue
Valerie Fitzgerald	Rei Mesa	Larry Vecchio
Wes Foster	Dewey Mitchell	Jim Weichert
De Ann Golden	Bob Molta	Bruce Zipf

ABOUT THE AUTHOR

Allan Dalton's deep industry-wide experience is reflected in **BUYER AGENT BE AWARE**. His resume includes being a former president and co-owner of a 50+ regional real estate brokerage, Murphy Realty Better Homes and Gardens, former Senior Vice President of NRT, former CEO of Realtor.com, past president of Move Inc. real estate division former president of Prominent Properties Sotheby's International Realty, co-founder of TownAdvisor, CEO of Real Living, Senior VP of Research & Development Berkshire Hathaway HomeServices, Senior VP of Research & Development HomeServices of America.

INDUSTRY ACHIEVEMENTS

Co-Author

ERA Selection and Development System
Leveraging Your Links
Creating Real Estate Connections
Real Estate Influence
34 Proclamations
Build a Bigger, Better& Profitable Real Estate Team

Creator of...

The Real Estate Financial Planning System
The Real Living Lifestyle Planning system
BHHS Real Estate Lifestyle Planning System Guide
Neighbors Know Best
Moving Children
Moving with Pets
Downsizing by Design
The Rent to Buy Assistance Program
The Holiday Home Marketing System
The Real Estate Outernet
Homes Guides in 6 languages
The 7 A's of Buyer-side Value

Created National Marketing Systems for...

Better Homes and Gardens
- Home Marketing System
- Home Buying System
- Home Information System

Century 21
- Custom Home Marketing System

ERA
- Value-Added Marketing System

The Coldwell Banker/NRT
- Full-Service Marketing System

Berkshire Hathaway HomeServices
- Customized Marketing System

Real Living
- Home Marketing System

Awards:

NAR's Realtor® Magazine – 25 Most Influential Thought Leaders
Swanepoel Power 200 Industry Leaders
RIS Media Hall of Fame
Book dedication from Mike Ferry
Better Homes & Garden's President's Award
(highest services award for the brand)

Dalton resides in Connecticut with his wife Carol, is the father of three daughters (Ginny, Becky & Laura), and is a proud grandfather to nine grandchildren. Dalton, who was named by Atlantic Magazine as "America's Best Pickup Player", was a former Boston Celtics draft choice, and remains active playing pickup basketball across America.

Learn More About
Ryan's Film Company,
Grayson Berry Productions

ABOUT THE EDITOR/DESIGNER

Thomas 'Ryan' Ward constantly contributes to collaborative projects worldwide – from film, theater, and concert productions to marketing, branding, and design consultation. In the past five years alone, Ryan has contributed to the creation of three feature films and two shorts, two film festivals, six original musicals, three professional theatrical companies, and four charitable events. When asked, Ryan shares that he derives his greatest joy from working with learners of all ages toward creating something amazing and unique… especially those with learning and developmental differences whom he has had the honor of collaborating with for over two decades with the VSA Arts of The Kennedy Center – which named Ryan one of only 5 Master Teaching Artists in the state of South Carolina in 2020.

Ryan would love to thank one of his favorite collaborators, the author of this book, Allan Dalton, for always including him in exciting projects and new concepts for the real estate industry… especially the work they have done together creating and producing "Real Estate Town Documentaries" (some of which you have seen within **BUYER AGENT BE AWARE**).

Should you, your team, or your company care to engage Allan and Ryan to produce these passionate town testimonials and lifestyle information-rich marketing products, contact us at allandaltonconsulting@gmail.com

Made in the USA
Las Vegas, NV
25 October 2024

10466040R00188